IN SOUTH AFRICAN WATERS
Passenger Liners Since 1930

IN SOUTH AFRICAN WATERS
Passenger Liners Since 1930

David Hughes
Peter Humphries

1977
Oxford University Press
Cape Town

Oxford University Press

Oxford London Glasgow
New York Toronto Melbourne Wellington
Ibadan Nairobi Dar es Salaam Lusaka Cape Town
Kuala Lumpur Singapore Jakarta Hong Kong Tokyo
Delhi Bombay Calcutta Madras Karachi

ISBN 0 19 570120 8
      0 19 570142 9 (De Luxe Edition)

Set in 10 pt on 12 pt Optima
by Photoprints, Twinell House, Loop Street, Cape Town
Printed and bound by Citadel Press, Polaris Road, Lansdowne, Cape
Published by Oxford University Press, Oxford House,
11 Buitencingle Street, Cape Town, South Africa

CONTENTS

ACKNOWLEDGEMENTS

The authors gratefully acknowledge the sources of the photographs used on the following pages:

Aitken, H. 27, 71, 90
Ashworth, Capt. 86
Authors' Collection 19, 36, 48, 129
British India Line 10-4
Burger, Die 50
Cape Archives 106-25, 127
Collins, C. 69
Company Postcards 7, 8, 16-8, 31-3, 38-41, 43, 49, 51, 52, 54, 60-4,
    67, 68, 76, 80-4, 87-9, 96, 98
Daily News 26, 59
Ellerman Lines 37
Farrell Line 45, 46
Harland & Wolff 99
Holland Africa Line 58
Rutherford, Capt. 3
Safmarine dust jacket, 103, 104
Shaw Savill Line 92, 94, 95, 97, 100, 101
World Ship Society 78
Young, George 2, 5, 6, 20-5, 29, 34, 35, 42, 56, 57, 66, 70, 73-5, 93,
    126, 128

FOREWORD

South Africans have always displayed extraordinary interest in passenger liners, so that their demise in recent times has come as something of a blow, not only for the would-be ocean traveller, but also for those people who peered, goggle-eyed, at the internal luxury and external graces of liners.

We live in a generation where sheer economic considerations have expunged splendid liners from the seven seas, probably never to be replaced.

It is useful, therefore, to be reminded of some of the liners of yore, and this volume, for the layman by laymen, provides easy reference to the many liners which, down the years, have plied the sea routes to and from South Africa.

The publication makes no pretence at being technical; the technical side of liners serving South Africa would be worthy of a volume all of its own. It does, though, include many interesting facts about the histories of the many liners.

As one who, for nearly half a century, was associated with the ships which sailed in and out of South African ports, I welcome this publication.

George Young
Shipping Editor, *The Cape Times*

INTRODUCTION

The last of the passenger liner services connecting South Africa with ports across the oceans has come to an end. Appropriately, the last sailing was taken by a vessel on the South African registry, the South African Marine Corporation's SA VAAL.

The first regular passenger liner service came into operation almost 157 years ago when the General Screw Steam Shipping Company sent their steamer BOSPHORUS out from England to the Cape. She sailed from England in December 1850 and arrived in Table Bay on 27 January 1851.

Many other shipping companies came into being and maintained regular passenger connections with many parts of the world. The advent of air travel, however, started the decline of the passenger liner, which accelerated after World War II. One by one, the passenger liner operators cut back their services until finally they ceased altogether.

Few people remember the famous liners of the past: the SCOT, the CARISBROOK CASTLE, rivals of the Union and Castle Mail Packets before amalgamation; Bucknall's FORT SALISBURY, BULUWAYO and JOHANNESBURG; the Portuguese LISBOA and LUSITANIA, both of which were wrecked on South Africa's coast, and the many other liners of companies long since defunct.

However, many people recall the passenger liners which called at our ports during the past 45 years or so, and the vessels of that period are recorded here.

Some familiar names are omitted because they were cruise ships and not liners in the strict sense. For the same reason no mention is made of troopships or 'Suez diverts'.

Many people contributed to this book; their stories and memories have been gratefully used. Some stories are, however, not included. Who would really want to know the identity of the mail steamer in which the soup was referred to, by an irate passenger, as 'bill poster's paste, variously coloured every day' or that another class of liner was so tender that the slightest sea set them going like the pendulum of a grandfather clock, to the discomfort of passenger and crew alike?

We must rather recall the good times. Few people who travelled in the old WINCHESTER CASTLE could forget the grandeur of the first and tourist class lounges, with their Spanish decor and comfortable wingbacked rockers. In the opinion of many, this ship and her sister, the WARWICK CASTLE, were the peak of ocean travel on the mail service. Then there was the magnificent service of the Goanese stewards in the Bullard, King 'Um' boats and Ellerman and

Bucknall's City liners, *la dolce vita* on the Italian vessels and the oompah bands and *Bierfeste* on the vessels of the German East Africa and Woermann lines. These vessels did not only provide a point-to-point service from South Africa to almost every point of the compass; they also gave jaded South Africans the opportunity for short coastal cruises. There was wining and dining and dancing 'til dawn, and for the less energetic, a deckchair in a quiet corner, a good book and no telephones. All this has been replaced by the container vessel.

We must record our thanks to the many people that we pestered during the compilation of this book: George Young, for the loan of numerous photographs and for the use of his large collection of Lloyd's Registers, extensively used in the checking of facts, particularly of the earlier liners; Henry Aitken, Clem Bauer, David Shackleton, Glyn Townley, Alec Young and other members of the Port Natal branch of the World Ship Society for their help and encouragement, Captain Ashworth of Royal Interocean Lines, Durban; and Captain Stephen Fox, late master of the Bank Line's INCO-MATI, of Cape Town; the various officials of many shipping companies whose patience in answering questions and digging up photographs was phenomenal; and all those who helped in one way or another, very often without knowing it.

DAVID HUGHES
PETER HUMPHRIES

BANK LINE

Andrew Weir and Company first entered the South Africa to India trade in 1906, using chartered tonnage. In 1913 they bought three old passenger vessels, the JOHANNESBURG, BULUWAYO and FORT SALISBURY, from the Bucknall Line. These they renamed SURAT, KATHIAWAR and GUJARAT and with them maintained a passenger service across the Indian Ocean. In 1924 the elderly liners were replaced by three new motor vessels, the second GUJARAT, the second KATHIAWAR and the LUXMI.

Andrew Weir's passenger service between India and Africa came to an end with the disposal in the mid 1960s of the INCHANGA and ISIPINGO, though their well known 'Bank' motor vessels, which carry no passengers, are still visitors to South African ports.

KATHIAWAR

These vessels were brought onto the India to South Africa run in the mid 1920s when many Indians living in South Africa were returning to India. The liners always turned at Cape Town, with calls at Durban and, sometimes, other coastal ports.

The KATHIAWAR was wrecked on a reef near Goa Island off northern Mozambique on 30 October 1937, while on a voyage to Durban. One of the cadets, Wilfred Koningkramer, who was trained in the SATS GENERAL BOTHA and was in his first ship, was commended later by the passengers for the manner in which he commanded his lifeboat after the passengers and crew had abandoned ship.

The other two vessels operated throughout World War II, and after the war returned to their normal service, though their passenger accommodation was removed and they operated as cargo-only vessels. In 1953 the GUJARAT was sold to the Cathay Shipping Co. Ltd., of Singapore, who renamed her EVERLIFE. The LUXMI remained in the Bank Line service until she was disposed of in 1962, the same year in which the Cathay Shipping Company disposed of the EVER-LIFE, ex-GUJARAT.

These vessels were not notable in any way except for their mainly trouble-free service. With their single squat funnel, common to so many motor vessels, their two masts and usual array of derricks and samson posts, they looked very much like so many other vessels of their type on the world's shipping lanes.

| GUJARAT | 4 148 grt | KATHIAWAR | 4 150 grt |
| LUXMI | 4 148 grt | | |

112,7m x 14,6m
Passengers carried in 1st class and tween decks.
Built: Harland and Wolff Ltd., Belfast, 1923, 1923, 1924.
Diesel engines, single screw, 12 knots.

These motor vessels were built by the Bank Line especially for their India to South and East Africa run, and were launched within two months of each other. They were very popular with ocean travellers to the East, and provided the height of low-cost luxury at the time.

The INCOMATI was slightly bigger and was the more powerful vessel. Whereas the other two had normal custom-built engines, those in the INCOMATI had previously been installed in the Furness liner BERMUDA, which had been burned out twice and was scrapped after the second disaster. These engines were bigger and more powerful, and gave the INCOMATI a knot or two beyond her service speed.

During World War II, all three were used on government service, and while ferrying the crew of a torpedoed vessel to Table Bay the INCOMATI was shelled and sunk by a U-boat in 1943. The sinking occurred off the island of S. Thome in the Gulf of Benin. Four of the lifeboats were destroyed during the attack. Seven other boats got away safely, the only casualty being a cook who had a heart attack while abandoning ship. Among the survivors was Major Bernard Cayzer, later to become vice-chairman of British and Commonwealth, the parent company of Union Castle and Clan Line.

The INCHANGA and ISIPINO survived the war and returned to their pre-war service in 1946. In the early fifties, after the passenger trade to India had fallen off, passenger accommodation was reduced to 12 passengers each.

Both vessels were disposed of for scrap in about 1966.

ISIPINGO

| INCHANGA ISIPINGO | 7 069 grt | 123,1m x 17,3m |
| INCOMATI | 7 369 grt | 127,4m x 17,3m |

Passengers carried in three classes.
Built: Workman, Clark (1928) Ltd., Glasgow, 1934.
Diesel engines, twin screw, 15 knots.

BLUE FUNNEL LINE

The vessels of Alfred Holt's Blue Funnel Line have been associated with South African ports for more than 100 years, but it was only in 1910 that the company entered the passenger trade around the Cape. In that year they started a six-weekly service from the United Kingdom to Australia via the Cape with the AENEAS, ANCHISES and ASCANIUS. Between the wars, the service was operated jointly first with the Aberdeen-White Star Line, and later with the Shaw Savill and Albion Line. This arrangement was not renewed after World War II, and the Blue Funnel Line operated independently from then until they ceased passenger operations in the mid 1960s.

The once-familiar blue funnel is very rarely seen in South African ports today.

These vessels, with their tall black-topped blue funnels and straight masts, were a familiar sight in South African ports, mainly Table Bay, in the years between the wars. They were then on the service run jointly by Shaw Savill and Albion and the Blue Funnel Line between the United Kingdom and Australia, going out and back via the Cape. They were sturdy and solid-looking vessels, but hardly beauties.

Two of this class were lost during World War II. The first, the AENEAS, was bombed 21 miles off Start Point on 2 July 1940, and sank two days later. She had been the biggest vessel in her convoy, which made her the obvious target for the German bombers. Nineteen lives were lost during the attack and when the vessel sank.

The ANCHISES was bombed and sunk by German bombers seven months later, on 27 February 1941, about 180 miles west-north-west of North Aran Isle, County Donegal, Eire. There were 156 survivors from this vessel and 16 lives were lost.

The ASCANIUS survived the war and continued in Blue Funnel service for a further four years until she was sold to the Cia de Nav Florentia SA, Italy, in 1949, who renamed her SAN GIOVANNINA. They operated her for less than three years and in 1952 she was broken up in Italy.

ASCANIUS

AENEAS	10 058 grt	ANCHISES	10 000 grt
ASCANIUS	10 048 grt	150m x 18m	

Passengers carried in one class only.
Built: Workman, Clark and Co., Belfast, 1910, 1911, 1910.
Triple expansion engines, coal burning, twin screw, 14 knots.

5

NESTOR

NESTOR 14 629 grt **ULYSSES** 14 647 grt

172m x 21m

Passengers carried in one class only.

Built: Workman, Clark and Co., Belfast, 1913.

Triple expansion engines, coal burning, twin screw, 14 knots.

There was never any mistaking the NESTOR or the ULYSSES. They had the tallest funnels of any vessel afloat, some 24,38 metres above the boat deck; they were straight up without any rake at all. The two vessels, though, could be distinguished from one another because the NESTOR's stem was straight while that of the ULYSSES was raked. Built for the Shaw Savill and Albion Blue Funnel joint service between the United Kingdom and Australia, via the Cape, both liners saw service in World War I as troopships. On their peacetime service, they were familiar sights in Table Bay between the wars. When World War II broke out neither vessel was considered suitable for trooping; their comparatively slow speed militated against such service. The ULYSSES, however, was requisitioned under the Liner Requisition Scheme. The wartime livery of grey all over could not hide the profiles of these two vessels, and the U-boat commander who got the ULYSSES in his periscope sight off Palm Beach, Florida, on 10 April 1942, must have known at a glance the class of vessel he was about to sink. There were no casualities when the ULYSSES went down.

The NESTOR was never taken up for war service and remained on her company's run to the Antipodes throughout the war. She was the only Blue Funneller not to be taken up for war service. After the end of the war, the NESTOR, back in her company livery of black hull, white superstructure and black-topped blue funnel, carried on in the service between England and Australia via the Cape, almost as if the war had never happened.

She left Cape Town on her last voyage in June 1950. At 38 years of age she had given good service but newer ships were coming forward. Later that year she arrived at Faslane on the Gareloch in Scotland where she was broken up.

During the 1930s until the outbreak of World War II these vessels often supplemented the Blue Funnel service between the United Kingdom and Australia, via the Cape. They were regular visitors to Table Bay during those years.

On the outbreak of war, the ANTENOR, HECTOR and PATROCLUS were converted into armed merchant cruisers. The ANTENOR served in this capacity until 1942 when she was converted for troop carrying. The PATROCLUS was the first of the quartet to come to grief. On 3 November, while in company with another armed merchant cruiser, the ex-White Star liner LAURENTIC, the latter vessel was hit by torpedoes from the U 99. The PATROCLUS stood by to pick up survivors but in doing so became a target for the U-boat which promptly torpedoed the ex-Blue Funneller. Three officers and 46 ratings died with the LAURENTIC; the PATROCLUS went down with the loss of 76 lives. The two vessels were about 190 miles west of Ireland at the time.

The HECTOR, 18 months later, was caught in Colombo harbour, Ceylon, when Japanese aircraft raided the area. The HECTOR was set alight and eventually sank. Her hulk was raised in 1946 and broken up. After the war, the SARPE-DON, the only one of the quartet not to have been commissioned in the Royal Navy, joined the NESTOR on the United Kingdom to Australia run until she was sold for scrap in 1953. The ANTENOR was disposed of for scrap in the same year.

HECTOR

| ANTENOR | 11 174 grt | HECTOR | 11 198 grt |
| PATROCLUS | 11 314 grt | SARPEDON | 11 321 grt |

152m x 19m

Passengers carried in one class only.
Built: Antenor — Palmer's Co. Ltd., Newcastle, 1925.
Hector/Patroclus — Scott's S.B. and E. Co. Ltd, Greenock, 1924/1923.
Sarpedon — Cammell, Laird and Co. Ltd, Birkenhead, 1923.
Steam turbines, twin screw, 15 knots.

7

PERSEUS

HECTOR	HELENUS	IXION	10 125 grt
JASON	10 160 grt		
PATROCLUS	PERSEUS	10 109 grt	
PELEUS	PYRRHUS	10 093 grt	

159,3m x 21,1m (Helenus class); 157,2m x 20,8m (Peleus class)
Passengers carried in first class only.
Built: Hector, Helenus, Ixion — Harland and Wolff Ltd., Belfast, 1950, 1949, 1951.
Jason — Swan Hunter and Wigham Richardson, Newcastle, 1950.
Patroclus, Perseus — Cammell, Laird and Co., Birkenhead, 1949.
Peleus, Pyrrhus — Vickers Armstrong Ltd., Newcastle, 1950.
Three steam turbines, single screw, 18,5 knots.

Alfred Holt's Blue Funnel Line laid down, among others, the HELENUS and PELEUS classes, each of four vessels, to replace passenger liners lost during World War II. The former class vessel was slightly bigger to allow for 3 500 tons of refrigerated cargo space. They were delivered between 1949 and 1951, and were put on the company's service between the United Kingdom and the Antipodes, out via the Cape and home variously via the Panama Canal, the Suez Canal or the Cape.

Though vessels of these two classes were also used on the company's other services, all eight vessels were seen in South African ports between 1949 and 1965 when the Blue Funnel Line ceased passenger-carrying operations. In that year the passenger accommodation in all their vessels was suppressed and the vessels became purely cargo carriers.

In June 1972 the JASON went to Taiwan for breaking up, and in the same month the IXION was delivered to Spanish shipbreakers. The others followed shortly afterwards, the PATROCLUS being the last to go — in 1973.

BRITISH INDIA LINE

The British India Steam Navigation Company was associated with the trade to and from South Africa for many years before it started a passenger service between South Africa and India in 1902. In that year it extended its service, which already came to Maputo, to take in Durban and Cape Town. Later the terminal port was set as Durban, and their ships rarely came as far south as Cape Town. For many years the company maintained a fortnightly mail and passenger service between Durban and Bombay, a service which came to an end with the last sailing of the KARANJA in 1976.

TAIREA

These vessels, two of a class of three, were originally built for the company's Calcutta to the Far East service, but were brought onto the Bombay to Durban, via the East African coast route in 1932 to replace the aging 'K' class vessels.

They had three funnels, one of which was a dummy, for the purpose of impressing the Chinese with the vessels' speed and power. They were among the smallest three-funnelled vessels ever built, and were the only such liners on regular service to South African ports.

Both plied the route regularly until the outbreak of World War II when the TAIREA was refitted as a hospital ship and the TAKLIWA as a troop transport. The wartime grey did very little for the appearance of the TAKLIWA but the white livery of a hospital ship showed off the lines of the TAIREA to great advantage. This may have been one of the reasons for the company's changing the livery of their vessels on the South African run after the war from the usual drab black hulls to white all over.

The TAIREA was present at the Madagascar landings, and both vessels were at Sicily, where the third of the trio, the TALAMBA, was sunk. Shortly after the war, while on a voyage to India from the Far East, the TAKLIWA went aground on Great Nicobar Island and later caught fire. The vessel was totally destroyed.

The TAIREA did not return to the Bombay to Durban run after the war but was instead returned to her original route until she was withdrawn from service in 1952 and sold for breaking up.

TAIREA   7 933 grt   **TAKLIWA**   7 936 grt
137m x 18m
Passengers carried in three classes.
Built: Barclay, Curle and Co. Ltd., Glasgow, 1924.
Triple expansion engines, coal burning, twin screw, 16 knots.

Built especially for the British India service from Bombay to East and South Africa, these two vessels, with the two 'T' class ships, maintained the service until the outbreak of World War II.

They carried passengers in first and second classes and also had accommodation for nearly 2 000 'deck' passengers, a facility for the conveyance of passengers between the many ports of East Africa in a service which did not always require passengers to spend the night on board the vessel.

At the outbreak of war, both vessels were taken up for trooping, and while serving in this role the KARANJA was sunk by enemy aircraft off Bougie, Algeria, on 12 November 1942.

The KENYA was converted to an infantry landing ship and was renamed HMS KERAN, to avoid confusion with the cruiser KENYA. She was at Madagascar in 1942 and in North Africa in 1943. Bought by the British Admiralty in 1946, she was sold to the Alva Steamship Co. Ltd. of London in 1949. Then began a process of renaming that left the ship world quite dizzy. Between 1949 and 1951 she was, in quick succession, renamed KENYA, KERAN, then back to KENYA, then FAIRSTONE – while laid up in Rothesay Bay – and back to KENYA, when moved to Holy Loch, and finally back to KERAN. In August 1951, she entered service once more – as the CASTEL FELICE for the Sitmar Line of Italy.

In this company's ownership she plied between Italy and Australia, Italy and South America, across the North Atlantic, and later from the United Kingdom to Australia. Flying the Italian flag for most of the time, she spent her last years on Panamanian registry, and was broken up in Taiwan in 1970.

The KENYA had a long and useful career, but is best remembered for the long series of unnecessary renamings halfway through her life.

KARANJA

KENYA   9 890 grt   **KARANJA**   9 891 grt
143m x 19,5m
Passengers carried in three classes.
Built: Alex Stephen and Sons Ltd., Glasgow, 1930, 1931.
Six steam turbines, coal burning, twin screw, 16 knots.

11

AMRA

Designed, with her original sister, the ASKA, for the Calcutta to Rangoon service, the AMRA made her maiden voyage in November 1938. The ASKA went out East the following year, but hardly had she arrived on her appointed route than World War II broke out. Both vessels were taken up for war service, the AMRA as a hospital ship and the ASKA as a troop transport. In September 1940, while she was bringing French troops from West Africa to Britain, the ASKA was attacked by a German bomber, hit three times and abandoned. Twelve civilians lost their lives but all the troops were saved. The ship drifted ashore and became a total wreck.

The AMRA, as a hospital ship, took part in the East African, the Sicilian and Italian campaigns.

To replace the ASKA, the company laid down the ARONDA which came into commission in 1941 as a troop ship. Her dimensions were similar to those of the AMRA and ASKA.

After the war, the Burmese service having been terminated, the two vessels were put on the route from India to East and South Africa. Originally coal burners, they were converted to oil fuel at Durban in 1950 by James Brown. This was the biggest contract of its kind undertaken by a South African shipbuilding firm up to that time. Offering first rate accommodation in two classes and able to take more than 2 000 deck passengers, the two vessels soon proved popular in the service. By the mid 1960s, however, the passenger trade had fallen off, and the two vessels were withdrawn. The ARONDA went first, in 1965, and the AMRA in December 1966, both for breaking up.

AMRA   8 314 grt   **ARONDA**   8 328 grt
140,4m x 18,7m
Passengers carried in three classes.
Built: Swan Hunter and Wigham Richardson Ltd., Newcastle, 1938, 1941.
Six steam turbines, coal burning, converted to oil 1950, twin screw, 16 knots.

The British India Company had suffered severe losses during World War II, and these two vessels were among their extensive war loss replacement programme. The first was named after the capital of Uganda; the second, the name of an island near Bombay, after the previous KARANJA which was lost in 1942.

The new vessels were not unlike in appearance to those that they were intended to replace, though they were in fact somewhat bigger and carried considerably more passengers. They soon became firm favourites among travellers between India and East and South Africa.

In 1969/70, they were refitted as one-class vessels with passengers carried in cabin and bunk accommodation.

At first they ran with the AMRA and ARONDA, and later with the new KENYA and UGANDA. As the passenger traffic declined, first the 'A' class went, and then the KENYA and UGANDA were withdrawn. As the trade had declined even further, the KAMPALA was withdrawn in 1972 and sold to Taiwanese shipbreakers. The KARANJA carried on alone for the next four years. In mid 1976 it was announced that she was to be withdrawn and that no replacement would be provided. With her departure from Durban came the end of the British India service from South Africa to India, a service which had started more than a century before.

KARANJA

KAMPALA   10 304 grt   **KARANJA**   10 294 grt
145,5m x 20,2m
Passengers carried in three classes.
Built: Alex Stephen and Sons Ltd., Glasgow, 1947, 1948.
Six steam turbines, twin screw, 16 knots.

13

KENYA

These two liners, among the last passenger vessels built for the British India Company, were designed specifically for the service between London and East Africa. In their early years of service they used to turn round at Beira in Mozambique and were not seen in South African ports. However, the first Suez crisis in 1956 changed this and they were forced to use the route round the Cape. After the Suez Canal was re-opened, the vessels returned to that route but often came down the east coast as far as Durban.

When the Suez Canal was closed again in 1967, the KENYA and UGANDA once more had to make use of the long route round the Cape. Because of the length of the voyage the service soon became uneconomical, despite the fact that the two vessels had been converted from first and tourist class into one-class ships in 1967, and in June 1969 the KENYA was taken out of service and sold for scrap. She was broken up at Spezia in Italy shortly afterwards.

The UGANDA was also taken off the East African service, but was used as a cruise ship and as a school ship for a short while, doing educational cruises in northern waters. It was not long, however, before she followed her sister into the limbo of ships 'that have passed'.

KENYA 14 434 grt **UGANDA** 14 430 grt
164,5m x 21,8m
Passengers carried in two classes, later in one class only.
Built: Barclay, Curle and Co. Ltd., Glasgow, 1951, 1952.
Six steam turbines, twin screw, 16 knots (could do 19 knots).

COMPANHIA COLONIAL DE NAVEGACAO

The Colonial Navigation Company, to give it its English
name, began operations in 1930 with a number of second-
hand vessels, and plied between Portugal and the Portuguese
colonies on the west and east coasts of Africa. It also operated services to Brazil and to Portuguese possessions in the
Far East. The passenger services of this company came to an
end after the 1974 coup in Portugal, though its cargo services
have been maintained. All but one of its passenger liners have
been disposed of.

JOAO BELO

Built for the Woermann Line's West African service, she was the third GERTRUD WOERMANN in that fleet, the previous two having been wrecked on the coast of South West Africa. In 1910 her name was changed to WINDHUK to free her first name for a new vessel which was just coming into service. This vessel was well known in Table Bay under both names, before World War I.

The outbreak of that war found the WINDHUK in Germany. After the Armistice, she was awarded to Britain as reparations and was sold in 1920 to Ellerman Lines who renamed her CITY OF GENOA. They operated her for eight years, and in 1928 she was bought by the new Portuguese Companhia Colonial de Navegacao (Colonial Navigation Company). She was renamed JOAO BELO.

In 1930 the Colonial Navigation Company started a service to the ports of Angola and Mozambique, and the JOAO BELO with the COLONIAL pioneered this route. She remained on this route for the rest of her commercial life. She was a familiar sight in Table Bay during World War II with the Portuguese flag painted large on her sides. In 1950, when new vessels were coming forward from the builders' yards, the JOAO BELO was withdrawn and sold to shipbreakers. She was still in good condition; her 45-year-old engines could still, depending on the energy of her stokers, make the 14 knots for which she was designed. The JOAO BELO, whose German origin could never be mistaken, had been a credit to her builders.

JOAO BELO, ex-City of Genoa, ex-Windhuk,
ex-Gertrud Woermann   6 365 grt   125,6m x 15,5m
Passengers carried in three classes.
Built: Blohm and Voss, Hamburg, 1905.
Triple expansion engines, coal burning, twin screw, 14 knots.

COLONIAL

Built as the YPIRANGA for the Hamburg Amerika Linie (Hapag), this neat little passenger liner was surrendered to the Allies in 1919, and sold the following year to the Anchor Line who renamed her ASSYRIA. They used her on their North Atlantic service until 1925. After a short period when laid up, the ASSYRIA went onto the Anchor Line's Bombay service, and was also used as a cruise ship. In 1929 she was sold to the Companhia Colonial.

Renamed COLONIAL, she was used by her new owners on their service from Lisbon to ports in Angola and Mozambique, calling at Cape Town on the outward and return voyages.

After 42 years under three flags and three owners, she was withdrawn from service and sold for breaking up. She was given her fourth and final name, BISCO 9, for the voyage from Lisbon to the breakers in 1950. She was, however, wrecked near Campbelltown, just short of her final destination, Dalmuir.

COLONIAL, ex-Assyria, ex-Ypiranga
8 072 grt   136,5m x 16,8m
Passengers carried in three classes.
Built: Fred Krupp, Kiel, 1908.
Quadruple expansion engines, coal burning, twin screw, 13,5 knots.

17

MOUZINHO

MOUZINHO, ex-Maria Christina, ex-Guglielmo Peirce, ex-Corcovado, ex-Sueh, ex-Corcovado

8 374 grt   136,5m x 16,8m

Passengers carried in three classes.

Built: Fred Krupp, Kiel, 1907.

Quadruple expansion engines, coal burning, twin screw, 13 knots.

Built as the CORCOVADO for the Hamburg South America Line, the MOUZINHO underwent several name changes before she was bought by the Colonial Navigation Company. She was awarded to Italy as part reparations after World War I, and was flying the Italian flag when, in 1929, she was bought by the Portuguese company.

She joined the JOAO BELO and COLONIAL in a three-ship service to Angola and Mozambique but, unlike those two vessels which were registered in Lisbon, the MOUZINHO was registered in the Angolan capital of Luanda.

Like her running mates, the MOUZINHO soon became popular with the South African travelling public who enjoyed the leisurely coastal voyages from Table Bay to Beira and return in these not too fast but very comfortable liners.

Their main purpose in life, though, was carrying the mail between Portugal and her overseas provinces, carrying garrison reliefs, and, of course, civil servants and settlers.

With the Portuguese flag painted on her sides, the MOUZINHO was a familiar and easily recognizable sight in Table Bay during World War II, but she did not continue long in the service after the war ended. In 1950, with two new and fast vessels coming from the builders' yards, the company disposed of the old vessels. The MOUZINHO, like her consorts, was sold to shipbreakers.

These two vessels were the first new ships built for the Colonial Navigation Company, as all their previous tonnage had been second-hand.

They were typical John Brown products, the PATRIA having come off the same slipway on which the QUEEN ELIZABETH had been built. The style of the stem and bows of the two Portuguese liners showed their family resemblance to the great Cunarder.

Their first class accommodation was luxurious for that type of vessel and both became popular with South African coastal tourists. They had their hard core of clientele, in the same way as their opposition, the ANGOLA and MOZAMBIQUE of the rival company, had theirs.

Both vessels gave satisfactory service throughout their careers, although the PATRIA broke down in Cape Town on her maiden voyage and spent several weeks there undergoing repairs, something that was not repeated. However, by 1972 their economical life was coming to an end; flying had taken away a lot of the passenger trade, and changes were looming in Africa. Both were sold, the PATRIA going to Taiwanese shipbreakers in June 1973, and the IMPERIO following her later that year.

PATRIA

PATRIA   13 196 grt   **IMPERIO**   13 186 grt
162m x 20,8m
Passengers carried in three classes.
Built: John Brown and Co., Clydebank, 1947, 1948.
Four steam turbines, twin screw, 17 knots.

19

INFANTE DOM HENRIQUE

INFANTE DOM HENRIQUE   23 306 grt   194,6m x 24,5m
Passengers carried in three classes.
Built: S.A. Cockerill-Ourgree, Hoboken, Belgium, 1961.
Four steam turbines, twin screw, 20 knots.

The largest and last passenger liner built for the Colonial Navigation Company, the INFANTE DOM HENRIQUE is also Portugal's largest-ever liner. Named after Prince Henry the Navigator, she was designed to ply the routes discovered by Prince Henry's explorers. Unfortunately, she was built too late; air travel had already gained the ascendancy when she took to the water on 20 April 1960, and it is doubtful if she ever paid for herself.

Her standard of accommodation was of the highest, and even her troops decks were much more comfortable than any previously known to the Portuguese soldier.

She was only 13 years old when she was withdrawn from service, a very short period for a vessel of her type. Unsuccessful as a mail liner, equally unsuccessful as a cruise ship, she was brought out of lay-up to help with the evacuation of Portuguese citizens after Mozambiquan and Angolan independence. She was then returned to her lay-up berth in Lisbon, where she remains: the pride of the Portuguese Merchant Navy; like the FRANCE of the French Merchant Navy, nobody wants her. It is a sad end to a fine vessel, and also to an efficient and comfortable ocean passenger service.

COMPANHIA NACIONAL DE NAVEGACAO

The Companhia Nacional de Navegacao's first regular appearance in a South African port was in 1906. The company, then called the Empreza Nacional de Navegacao, was operating a service between Lisbon and the Portuguese territories in Africa. In 1918, the old company was wound up and reformed as the National Navigation Company; same ships, same service, new name.

The Cia Nacional had a monopoly of the route for many years until 1930 when the Colonial Navigation Company appeared on the scene. The passenger services of the company were wound up after the Portuguese overseas territories became independent in 1974 and 1975. All the company's passenger vessels have since been disposed of, for scrap or to new owners.

LOURENCO MARQUES

LOURENCO MARQUES, ex-Admiral   6 298 grt

128m x 15m
Passengers carried in three classes.
Built: Blohm and Voss, Hamburg, 1905.
Triple expansion engines, coal burning, twin screw, 14 knots.

On the German East Africa Line's service until the start of World War I, the ADMIRAL was homeward bound from Durban when war broke out. She took refuge in Delagoa Bay at once, but in 1916, when Portugal entered the war on the side of the Allies, she was taken over and given to the Portuguese government shipping company under the name LOURENCO MARQUES.

Two years later the vessel was bought by the National Navigation Company who did not change her name, and was put into service on their route to Angola and Mozambique. She remained in this service for the next 33 years.

She was a comfortable vessel; her first and second class accommodation was reasonable for the period and popular with coastal tourists when berths were available. Her third class was, to say the least, spartan, and was used mainly for the transport of troops between Portugal and her overseas provinces.

With the arrival on the route of new ships after World War II, the LOURENCO MARQUES became surplus to requirements, and in 1951 she was disposed of for breaking up. She was then 46 years old, by any standards a great age for a passenger liner.

NYASSA

One of a class of vessels built for the Nord Deutsche Lloyd's Far East and Australia service and named after famous German field marshals and generals, the BÜLOW took refuge in Lisbon when World War I started. She was taken over by the Portuguese when that country joined the Allies in 1916 and was renamed TRAS-OS-MONTES. She was operated at first by the state shipping company, but after the war was sold to the National Navigation Company, who renamed her NYASSA — after one of the provinces in Mozambique — and put her on their mail run to Angola and Mozambique.

A comfortable and reliable vessel, her engines could still give 14 knots at the end of her life as against the 15 knots for which she was designed. During World War II she was one of the neutral vessels calling at South African ports which were able to provide tired South Africans with a short coastal cruise.

She was withdrawn from service in 1952 and broken up in Taiwan.

NYASSA, ex-Tras-os-Montes, ex-Bülow   8 980 grt
140,8m x 17,4m
Passengers carried in three classes.
Built: J.C. Tecklenborg AG, Wesermunde, 1906.
Quadruple expansion engines, coal burning, twin screw, 14 knots.

ANGOLA

ANGOLA, ex-Albertville   7 884 grt   134m x 17m
Passengers carried in three classes.
Built: S.A. John Cockerill, Hoboken, Belgium, 1912.
Quadruple expansion engines, coal burning, twin screw, 14 knots.

One of two vessels bought by the National Navigation Company from the Compagnie Maritime Belge in 1933 to counter the competition of the newly formed Colonial Navigation Company, the ANGOLA was very much like the other ships of the company in accommodation and service. She was not as frequent a caller as the other vessels of the company except during World War II. In 1947, to free her name for one of the new vessels then being built in Newcastle, her name was changed to NOVA LISBOA, but she did not carry that name for long; in 1952 she was disposed of for scrap.

The other vessel bought at the same time was the MOZAMBIQUE, ex-BRUXELLESVILLE, 5 771 grt. She was hardly ever seen in South African waters, and the company disposed of her about four years after she was bought.

QUANZA

When, in the late 1920s, the National Navigation Company decided to build a new ship, their first new building since before World War I, their choice of builders fell on Blohm and Voss because of the good service they had had from the ex-German vessels then in their fleet.

The new vessel, which was the first in the fleet to have a cruiser stern, was laid down as the PORTUGAL but the name was changed before she was commissioned.

A typical product of Blohm and Voss, she was a steady and comfortable vessel — even her third class was above the standard of that in the other vessels — and soon became a firm favourite among South Africa coastal tourists. In the days before air travel, the coastal cruise from Cape Town to Beira and back was very popular, and the QUANZA offered good value for money on this run. The QUANZA was not withdrawn when the new ships came out in 1948, but remained in the service with them until about 1968. She was then taken out of service and sold for scrap. Nearly 40 years old, she had given her owners good service.

QUANZA, ex-Portugal   6 517 grt   133,6m x 16m
Passengers carried in three classes.
Built: Blohm and Voss, Hamburg, 1929.
Triple expansion engines, coal burning, twin screw, 14 knots.

MOZAMBIQUE

After World War II the fleet of the National Navigation Company was aging; only the QUANZA was a relatively modern vessel, and new tonnage was necessary if the company was to maintain its services. They placed an order for two large motor vessels in England.

The ANGOLA came out first, and immediately made an impression on the South African travelling public. The MOZAMBIQUE followed shortly afterwards and soon joined her sister in that popularity. Their accommodation was far and away superior to anything the company had provided before. Even in the third class, where the advance was less marked, things were better than they had been in the older vessels. Anyway, South African tourists never travelled third class!

At first the two vessels called only at Cape Town, but later changed their port of call to Durban only. The popularity of the coastal cruises caused the company to make calls at both ports, outward and homeward.

The company's livery had always been a grey hull, white upper works, and a plain black funnel. A change was made shortly before the service came to an end, and the vessels came out with a blue funnel with a black top to it. This made a great change to the appearance of the vessels, a change for the better. However, it came too late because independence was imminent.

Trade fell off badly, and in 1972 the two vessels, after very short careers for Portuguese passenger liners, made their respective ways to the shipbreakers' yards.

ANGOLA   12 975 grt   **MOZAMBIQUE**   12 976 grt
167,5m x 20,5m
Passengers carried in three classes.
Built: Hathorn, Leslie and Co., Newcastle, 1948, 1949.
Doxford diesels, twin screw, 17 knots.

PRINCIPE PERFEITO

This imposing and handsome liner was the last, largest and fastest passenger vessel built for the National Navigation Company. She came out in the early 1960s when it was thought that trade to the African provinces of Portugal was expanding. The future of the PRINCIPE PERFEITO (Perfect Prince) was thought to be assured.

Stabilized and air conditioned, she had accommodation equal to that in any other vessel of her size and age, and superior to most. She had a good cargo capacity, and if necessary, she could carry troops with a little modification.

Independence in the Portuguese African provinces altered all that. With a glut of passenger liners on other routes, and the ever increasing competition from air travel, the PRINCIPE PERFEITO's future was bleak. After several voyages carrying refugees from Angola and Mozambique, she was withdrawn and put up for sale. Perhaps it was her air conditioning that saved her from the fate which had befallen her opposite number in the Colonial fleet, the INFANTE DOM HENRIQUE, because she has been sold to an unnamed buyer who is using her as a hostel ship in the Persian Gulf, now named AL HASA. After a little more than 14 years of service, she was too good to go to the shipbreakers.

With the withdrawal of the PRINCIPE PERFEITO, a service begun nearly 90 years ago came to an end.

PRINCIPE PERFEITO   19 393 grt   190,5m x 24m
Passengers carried in two classes.
Built: Swan Hunter and Wigham Richardson Ltd., Newcastle, 1961.
Four steam turbines, twin screw, 20 knots.

ELDER DEMPSTER LINE

Elder, Dempster and Company have been associated with the South African trade since 1906, when, with two other companies, they formed the Canadian — South African Line. The vessels they operated were freighters only, and it was not until the outbreak of World War II that the company entered the passenger trade. Because of the need for expatriates to take their leave away from the climate of West Africa, the company, which had for many years been operating passenger liners between West Africa and the United Kingdom, started a service between Cape Town and West African ports. This service was maintained for several years after the end of World War II, but when they withdrew their vessel in 1953 the service lapsed. It had been the only regular passenger service between South Africa and West Africa during the period under review.

In 1940, when expatriate civil servants and other people employed on the West Coast of Africa were unable to take their leave in the United Kingdom because of the war, the Elder Dempster Line started a passenger service from West Africa to Cape Town. For the service they used the CALABAR which had been designed for the Nigerian coastal trade.

Her trim lines soon became a familiar sight in Table Bay, and after the war ended, her owners decided to retain her on the route. She was refitted in Belfast and from then until 1953, maintained a regular monthly passenger and cargo connection between Table Bay and West Africa.

Her comfortable, while not luxurious, accommodation made her a firm favourite among clientele who preferred a quiet holiday on the water. She was not too fast, and she visited some very interesting ports in an interesting part of the world, away from the beaten track of the better known shipping companies. Many South Africans, after the war, did the round trip in the CALABAR as a voyage to 'there and back'.

In 1953 the CALABAR was sold to Worldwide Steamship Co. Inc., of Monrovia, and renamed SEMIRAMIS for service in the Mediterranean. The following year her registered owners were named as the Epirotiki Steamship Navigation Co., and her port of registry as Piraeus. Her tonnage had been increased to 2 269 grt, suggesting structural alterations.

She was still registered under the same owners and port of registry in the 1975-76 edition of Lloyd's Register.

The CALABAR was the smallest passenger line of her time in the South African trade.

CALABAR

CALABAR   1 932 grt   76m x 12,5m
Passengers carried in one class only.
Built: Harland and Wolff Ltd., Belfast, 1935.
Diesel engines, single screw, 12 knots.

ELLERMAN LINES

Through the old Bucknall Line, the Ellerman Lines have a long association with the South African passenger trade, going back to 1891. In 1914, Sir John Ellerman, having obtained a controlling interest in the Bucknall Line some years before, changed the name of the company to Ellerman and Bucknall Line, the name by which it was known in the South African trade until quite recently. Ellerman 'City' liners were familiar visitors to South African ports between the wars, and were among the most popular passenger liners in the trade.

After World War II, in their war replacement programme, four motor vessels were built specifically for the South African trade. Very popular, they were among the last passenger liners, apart from the regular mail vessels, to be withdrawn.

The cargo vessels of the Ellerman fleet are still regular visitors to South African ports.

The CITY OF LONDON had probably the most varied career of any of the passenger liners in the Ellerman fleet. Built for the India service of the City Line, she served as an armed merchant cruiser during World War I. The two 6-pounder anti-aircraft guns she carried were among the first fitted in an armed merchantman. She was released and returned to her owners in 1919, and after a thorough refit, was put back on the passenger run to India.

During the 1930s, when the passenger trade between the United Kingdom and India declined, the CITY OF LONDON was transferred to the South African run. She remained in this service until the outbreak of World War II.

During World War II the CITY OF LONDON was used in much the same way as most vessels of her age and potential. Towards the end of the war, though, she was used as an accommodation vessel for submarine crews in the Far East.

She was returned to her owners after the war but age and the ravages of wartime service had taken their toll. She was sold for scrap on 13 May 1946.

A sister, the CITY OF PARIS, also built in 1907, was sunk by a U-boat in the Mediterranean on 4 April 1917, with the loss of 122 lives.

The CITY OF LONDON was notable because of her strong resemblance to the Blue Anchor liner WARATAH which went missing off the South African coast in 1909. The similarity between the tonnages, lines, dimensions and general arrangements of the two liners has often been quoted by those who do not favour the theory that the WARATAH was top heavy. A point to note in this respect is that the WARATAH disappeared on her second voyage; the CITY OF LONDON was 39 years old when sold for scrapping.

CITY OF LONDON

CITY OF LONDON   8 956 grt   147,7m x 17,6m
Passengers carried in two classes, later in one class only.
Built: Workman, Clarke and Co. Ltd., Belfast, 1907.
Quadruple expansion engines, coal burning, 15 knots.

CITY OF MARSEILLES

CITY OF MARSEILLES   8 317 grt   143m x 17,4m
Passengers carried in two classes, later in one class only.
Built: Palmer's Co. Ltd., Newcastle, 1913.
Quadruple expansion engines, originally coal burning but later converted to oil, twin screw, 14 knots.

The CITY OF MARSEILLES was built for the Hall Line's service to India and was transferred to the South African run some time before World War II. She was wrecked off Ceylon in 1943 while on war service.

CITY OF EXETER

Built originally for the City Line's India service, the CITY OF EXETER was transferred to the South African service of Ellerman and Bucknall in 1933. She soon became a popular vessel on this run and remained on it until the end of her commercial life. The CITY OF EXETER was one of the first Ellerman liners to be fitted with a cruiser stern, something quite uncommon in 1914.

In 1939, shortly before the outbreak of World War II, the CITY OF EXETER was chartered by the British government to take a high level trade delegation to Russia. Shortly after her return she was given her wartime livery of grey, her uniform for the next seven years. Her wartime career was uneventful in the main. One of her last duties before returning to her owners was to take ex-King Zog of Albania and his family to Port Said after the Communist rulers of his country refused him leave to return to Tirrana, his capital.

The CITY OF EXETER was refitted and returned to the South African passenger run in 1946. From then until 1950 she carried many new South Africans to their country of adoption. In 1950, however, new vessels were in the offing and she was withdrawn. On 11 July that year she was sold for scrapping.

CITY OF EXETER   9 654 grt   148,4m x 18m
Passengers carried in two classes, later in one class only.
Built: Workman, Clark and Co. Ltd., Belfast, 1914.
Quadruple expansion engines, coal burning, later converted to oil, twin screw, 14 knots.

CITY OF CAIRO

CITY OF CAIRO   8 034 grt   137,1m x 17m
Passengers carried in two classes, later in one class only.
Built: Earle's Co. Ltd., Hull, 1917.
Quadruple expansion engines, coal burning, single screw, 14 knots.

Built during World War I, the CITY OF CAIRO was employed on the Hall Line's service to India and later on the South African service of Ellerman and Bucknall. On 6 November 1942, while on a voyage from Table Bay to Pernambuco in Brazil, she was torpedoed and sunk off St Helena Island with the loss of 82 of her crew and 22 passengers.

CITY OF BARODA

Originally on the Indian run, the CITY OF BARODA came onto the Hall Line's South African service later. She was torpedoed near Lüderitz Bay in South West Africa on 2 April 1943, with the loss of one of her crew and 13 passengers. The CITY OF BARODA remained afloat for some time after being torpedoed and later drifted ashore where she became a total wreck. The wreck was discovered some time after the disaster by a patrolling aircraft. This vessel figures in Geoffrey Jenkins' novel *A Bridge of Magpies*.

CITY OF BARODA   7 129 grt   132,1m x 17,4m
Passengers carried in two classes, later in one class only.
Built: Barclay, Curle and Co. Ltd., Glasgow, 1918.
Triple expansion engines, coal burning, single screw, 14 knots.

35

CITY OF SIMLA

CITY OF SIMLA   10 138 grt   148,3m x 17,7m
Passengers carried in two classes, later in one class only.
Built: Wm. Gray and Co. (1918) Ltd., West Hartlepool, 1921.
Four steam turbines, oil burning, twin screw, 13,5 knots.

The CITY OF SIMLA was one of the City Line's Indian 'Cities' but was later transferred to the Ellerman and Bucknall service to South Africa. She was well known in South African ports before World War II. She was one of the earliest losses among the company's passenger fleet when, on 21 September 1940, she was torpedoed and sunk about 50 miles north west of Malin Head in the Hebrides.

THE CITY OF PARIS, after 14 years on the Indian service, was brought onto the South African run in 1936. She was the first ship to be damaged by a magnetic mine in World War II. She survived the ordeal, was repaired and put back into service.

In 1942 the CITY OF PARIS was used in the exchange of diplomats after Japan's entry into the war, taking the Japanese diplomatic staffs to the point of exchange. She continued in service as a civilian transport until 1944 when she was taken in hand for conversion to a personnel ship for the Far East Fleet Train. Her conversion was not completed in time for her to join the Fleet Train, and instead, she was used as a floating barracks at Hong Kong for a while after the war.

She returned to normal service after the war. In 1948 she was given a thorough refit from which she emerged with a new appearance. Her tall straight funnel had been replaced with a streamlined one with a sloping top. Her appearance was greatly improved by this modification and she continued in service for a further seven years. Passenger demand, however, had dropped by the middle of the 1950s, and on 25 February 1956, the CITY OF PARIS was sold for scrapping. She was dismantled in Newport, Monmouthshire.

CITY OF PARIS

CITY OF PARIS   10 138 grt   148,3m x 17,7m
Passengers carried in two classes, later in one class only.
Built: Swan Hunter and Wigham Richardson, Newcastle, 1922.
Three steam turbines, coal burning, converted to oil burning in 1924, single screw, 15 knots.

CITY OF NAGPUR

CITY OF NAGPUR   10 146 grt   143,3m x 18,1m
Passengers carried in two classes, later in one class only.
Built: Workman, Clark and Co. Ltd., Belfast, 1922.
Quadruple expansion engines, oil burning, single screw, 14 knots.

Another of the Indian 'Cities', the CITY OF NAGPUR was well known in South African ports for some time before she was transferred to the South African service of Ellerman and Bucknall when the Indian passenger service declined during the 1930s. She had often taken sailings for that branch of the Ellerman group while still a unit of the Indian service. A comfortable vessel, she was popular with the South African travelling public.

The CITY OF NAGPUR did not survive World War II. She was torpedoed in the North Atlantic on 29 April 1941, when some 700 miles west of Ireland. Two of her gunners, 13 lascars and one of her passengers lost their lives when the vessel went down.

The CITY OF NAGPUR was one of the earlier cruiser sterned vessels at a time when counter sterns were still the vogue.

CITY OF CANTERBURY

The CITY OF CANTERBURY shared the popularity enjoyed by all Ellerman passenger liners on the South African service. During World War II she was taken up as a troop transport, being fitted to carry 1 500 troops each voyage, almost 10 times as many as passengers she carried during peacetime. She was at Crete during the Greek campaign and later carried the Greek Royal Family, together with the Crown Jewels, to South Africa after the fall of that country.

The CITY OF CANTERBURY was later used to carry South African troops to the Middle East, and was present at the invasion of Normandy on 6 June 1944.

She returned to normal service after the war ended and was withdrawn from service and sold for scrapping in 1953.

CITY OF CANTERBURY   8 331 grt   136,7m x 17,2m
Passengers carried in two classes, later in one class only.
Built: Swan Hunter and Wigham Richardson, Newcastle, 1922.
Quadruple expansion engines, coal burning, single screw, 14 knots.

39

CITY OF VENICE

CITY OF VENICE   8 762 grt   138,7m x 17,7m
Passengers carried in two classes, later in one class only.
Built: Workman, Clark and Co. Ltd., Belfast, 1924.
Quadruple expansion engines, oil burning, single screw, 14 knots.

The CITY OF VENICE was a unit of the City Line in their service to India but was also used in the South African service of Ellerman and Bucknall, on which route she was used almost continuously in the 1930s.

On the outbreak of World War II in 1939, the CITY OF VENICE was taken over as a transport, and on 4 July 1943, while bound for Sicily shortly after the invasion of that island by the Allies, she was torpedoed and sunk in the central Mediterranean. She was carrying military personnel and equipment at the time. Eleven of her crew and an unknown number of her military passengers were lost when she sank.

CITY OF HONG KONG

The CITY OF HONGKONG ran in the Ellerman and Buck-nall service until 1936 when she was transferred to the City Line. She was on the South African service when World War II broke out in 1939, and she was taken up under the Liner Requisition Scheme. Used as a transport for most of the war, she was returned to her owners when hostilities ended and was put back on the Ellerman service to South Africa. With new vessels coming forward from builders' yards, the CITY OF HONGKONG was withdrawn from service in 1951 and sold to Fratelli Grimaldi of Italy. Her new owners renamed her CENTAURO and operated her for a few years. In 1955 she was sold for scrap and broken up in Savona.

CITY OF HONGKONG   9 579 grt   143,1m x 18,7m
Passengers carried in two classes, later in one class only.
Built: Earle's Co. Ltd., Hull, 1924.
Quadruple expansion engines, oil burning, single screw, 15 knots.

CITY OF BENARES

The CITY OF BENARES was the only twin-funnelled vessel ever built by the Ellerman group; she was the first passenger liner laid down by the company for 12 years; and at the time of her building was the biggest passenger liner in the fleet.

She was built for the Indian trade via the Suez Canal, but was transferred to the South African service about two years before the outbreak of World War II. In the short time that she was on the South African run, she established a reputation as a comfortable and popular vessel.

The CITY OF BENARES' wartime career was tragically short. In September 1940, she embarked 191 passengers for the United States, among whom were 90 children who were being evacuated under the auspices of the Children's Overseas Reception Board, and nine adult escorts. On the night of 17 September, when about 600 miles out, the vessel was struck by a torpedo and sank very rapidly. The weather was rough, and difficulty was experienced lowering the lifeboats, some of which were swamped. Many people went down with the CITY OF BENARES and more died of exposure in the boats on that bitterly cold North Atlantic night. Of the 406 crew and passengers who left the United Kingdom in the vessel, 248 were lost, including 77 of the children and five of the escorts.

The sinking of the CITY OF BENARES brought to an end the scheme to evacuate British children to safety abroad.

CITY OF BENARES   11 081 grt   148,1m x 18,9m
Passenger carried in one class only.
Built: Barclay, Curle and Co. Ltd., Belfast, 1936.
Three steam turbines, twin screw, 15 knots.

CITY OF PORT ELIZABETH

This class of motor passenger liner was laid down in the early 1950s to replace the aging pre-war liners which were coming to the end of their economical lives. They were also the last passenger liners ordered by the Ellerman group.

They plied the route between the United Kingdom and South Africa for almost 20 years before the drop in demand for sea passages forced their withdrawal. They did the voyage from London to Cape Town in 15 days; their accommodation and service were of the highest standard. The announcement of their withdrawal was received with great regret by many who prefer an ocean voyage to a journey in an aircraft.

During 1971, as each vessel arrived back in London, it was taken out of service. The four vessels were sold to the Mediterranean-based Greek company of Karageorgis, who renamed them MEDITERRANEAN ISLAND, MEDITERRANEAN SEA, MEDITERRANEAN SKY and MEDITERRANEAN DOLPHIN respectively. They were converted to roll on/roll off style passenger and car ferries, and now sail between Italy, Greece and the Greek and Aegean islands.

CITY OF PORT ELIZABETH	13 363 grt	CITY OF EXETER	13 345 grt
CITY OF YORK	13 345 grt	CITY OF DURBAN	13 345 grt

164,9m x 21,7m.
Passengers carried in one class only.
Built: Vickers Armstrong Ltd., Newcastle, 1952, 1953, 1953, 1954.
Doxford diesels, twin screw, 16 knots.

43

FARRELL LINES

Known as the American – South African Line until shortly after World War II, Farrell Lines started their service to South Africa from the eastern seaboard of the United States more than 50 years ago. Always operating 12-passenger vessels, the company operated one regular passenger liner before World War II. This operation was sufficiently successful for the company to acquire two liners of similar passenger carrying capabilities after the war. They were on the service for several years until financial considerations, delays on the east coast of Africa among them, forced their withdrawal.

The company still operates freighters with accommodation for 12 passengers, always a very popular form of ocean transport.

The CITY OF NEW YORK was unusual in many ways. Not only was she the only passenger liner plying between the United States and South Africa before World War II, but she was more unusual in being a motor vessel, a form of propulsion not very popular among American ship owners.

The career of the CITY OF NEW YORK was uneventful but she provided travellers with first class accommodation, comfortable cabins and a good menu.

With one squat buff funnel, unadorned by the Farrell emblem as are the vessels today, she was no beauty, but the service she gave her owners until the attack on Pearl Harbour and America's entry into the war gave them no cause to complain.

After the United States came into the war, the CITY OF NEW YORK remained on the run between New York and South Africa until, on 29 March 1942, when 30 miles east of Cape Hatteras, she was struck by two torpedoes and sank with the loss of 16 lives. Her survivors were picked up by the US Coast Guard and taken to port. No passenger liner worked between the United States and South Africa for eight years.

CITY OF NEW YORK

CITY OF NEW YORK 8 272 grt 137,4m x 18,8m
Passengers carried in one class only.
Built: Sun Shipbuilding and Drydock Co., Chester, Pa. 1930.
Diesel engines by her builders, twin screw, 14 knots.

AFRICAN ENTERPRISE

AFRICAN ENDEAVOR   7 966 grt
AFRICAN ENTERPRISE   7 922 grt   142,6m x 20,1m
Passengers carried in one class only.
Built: Bethlehem Shipyard, Sparrows Point, Baltimore, Md, 1940.
Steam turbines, single screw, 16,5 knots.

These two vessels were built originally for the Delta Line and were launched as the DELBRASIL and DELARGENTINA respectively. They ran in the Delta Line's South American service until 1942 when they were requisitioned by the United States government for service as troop transports, and given the names GEORGE F ELLIOT and J W McANDREW respectively.

In 1946 they reverted to their original names, but two years later were given back their wartime names. They were bought by Farrell Lines in 1949 and given the names by which they were known on the South African seaboard. When taken over from the United States government the two vessels were in a sorry state, and an almost total rebuilding was necessary. This, however, allowed their new owners to fit them out as two of the most luxurious vessels of their type in service to South Africa. They boasted first class accommodation for 82 passengers, the public rooms were tastefully decorated, and the cuisine was of a high standard.

In appearance, though, they were thought to look top-heavy, their large high funnels contributing to this illusion, being big in proportion to the rest of the vessel. Their sterns were unusual in being half-counter, half-cruiser and unlike any other on a vessel then plying to South African ports. Generally, though, their profiles were not unpleasing. They were also among the very few single screw vessels calling at South African ports in the post-World War II years.

The passenger service between South Africa and the United States did not prove as successful as Farrell Lines had hoped, delays on the coast and particularly in Mozambique's ports contributing to a large degree. By 1959, the company decided that the vessels were not paying their way; and they were withdrawn and disposed of. Since then, travellers wishing to go to the United States by sea had had to make use of the 12-passenger vessels of the company.

GERMAN AFRICA LINES

Though by far the older of the two companies in the German Africa Lines, the Woermann Line was the second to come into the South African trade. Its first vessels arrived in Cape Town during 1898. The German East Africa Line (DOAL), founded only in 1890, called at Cape Town and Durban on their way to German East Africa (Tanganyika) from that year.

Having lost their entire fleets during and after World War I, the two companies operated a rationalized service from Germany to the former colonies between the wars, the liners, with few exceptions, bearing names beginning with W for Woermann and U for DOAL vessels.

Again, during and after World War II, the companies lost their entire fleets either by destruction or capture. After World War II neither company re-entered the passenger trade, and concentrated on freighters with limited passenger accommodation, usually for 12 passengers.

The German passenger liner service, up to the outbreak of World War II, was among the most popular with South African ocean travellers. This popularity has carried through to the company's present 12-passenger vessels which are frequent visitors to South African ports.

TOLEDO

TOLEDO, ex-Algeria, ex-Kigoma   8 123 grt

136m x 17m

Passengers carried in three classes.

Built: Reihersteig, Hamburg, 1914.

Quadruple expansion engines, coal burning, single screw, 13,5 knots.

The TOLEDO, though owned by the Hamburg Amerika Linie (Hapag), is included here because she was operated by the German Africa Lines during the last years of her career, and because she was originally a unit of the German East Africa Line fleet.

Built shortly before the outbreak of World War I as the KIGOMA for the German East Africa Line, she was a typical product of the period with her single funnel, two masts and counter stern. Comfortable and steady, she seemed set for a long and uneventful career on the African coast, but this was not to be. She had completed only one voyage when the war broke out.

In Hamburg at the time, the KIGOMA was taken up as a transport and used to ferry soldiers to the Russian front. Later she was fitted out to carry 9 000 troops for the projected invasion of the British Isles, an event which, of course, never materialized.

In 1918, with Germany in a state of mutiny, she was seized by mutineers and taken to Kiel where, it is said, her first class lounge was used as a 'court room' by mutineers trying 'offenders'. The story that her yard arms were used for executions was never confirmed.

After the war ended, the KIGOMA was taken over by the Allies and was awarded to Britain as reparations. In 1920 she was bought by the Anchor Line who renamed her ALGERIA. They used her for only two years and then put her up for sale. The ALGERIA was bought by Hapag in December 1922. They gave her her third name, TOLEDO, and put her on their Central America and West Indies service. Four years later she returned to the service for which she had been designed.

The TOLEDO was withdrawn from service during the depression in the early 1930s and was laid up. With no end to the depression in sight in 1934, she was sold to Italian shipbreakers and dismantled. She was just 20 years old.

This class of three vessels was the first ordered by the German Africa Lines to replace losses sustained during and after World War I. The first two were for the German East Africa Line and the WANGONI was to Woermann account. The USARAMO was the first to be delivered and enter service.

Single-funnelled with two masts and a counter stern, they were slightly smaller than the TOLEDO, ex-KIGOMA, but were otherwise a modification of that design. They used oil fuel instead of coal as in the older vessel.

They were graceful and comfortable vessels, and soon established a reputation on the African coast. Their careers, however, were not spectacular; they were just comfortable vessels which gave value for money.

The outbreak of World War II found the USSAKUMA abroad and the other two vessels in their home port. The USSAKUMA was stopped by a British cruiser off Bahia, Brazil, late in 1939. Her crew scuttled the vessel to avoid capture.

A similar fate overtook the USARAMO in 1944, when the retreating German Navy scuttled her in Bordeaux harbour where she was at the time of the Normandy invasion. After the war she was brought up and dismantled.

The WANGONI was in the Baltic towards the end of the war and fell into the hands of the advancing Russians in 1945. They renamed her CHUKOTKA and incorporated her into their Black Sea merchant fleet. She was last listed in Lloyd's Register under that name in 1967, by which time she was 47 years old. It is presumed that she has been scrapped.

WANGONI

| USARAMO | 7 775 grt | USSAKUMA | 7 834 grt |
| WANGONI | 7 849 grt | 122m x 17m | |

Passengers carried in three classes.
Built: Blohm and Voss, Hamburg, 1920.
Four steam turbines, single screw, 14 knots.

WAHEHE

These two neat looking little vessels, built for the Woermann Line, were smaller editions of the WANGONI class. They were the smallest of the German Africa Lines' vessels but were not the least in comfort or in popularity. They operated on the company's African services, with occasional diversions to the Seychelles, Mauritius and other islands off Africa, until the outbreak of war in 1939. The start of the war found the WADAI in Germany, and the WAHEHE trying to make a run for a friendly port. Luck, however, was not with the WAHEHE and she was captured by a British cruiser early in 1940. She was declared prize of war and taken over by the British Ministry of War Transport who handed to P. Henderson and Company to manage and operate on their behalf.

Renamed EMPIRE CITIZEN, she was employed on the North Atlantic service when, on 2 February 1941, she was torpedoed by a U-boat and sunk with the loss of her captain and 77 of her crew. The WADAI was taken over by Britain at the end of the war and renamed EMPIRE YARE. Later she was allocated to Russia as part of her reparations and joined the Soviet merchant fleet as the GOGOL, under which name she was still listed in 1976. She is employed as a training ship and operates from the port of Petropavlovsk Kamchatskiy on the Bering Strait coast of Siberia. At 55 years of age, the GOGOL, ex-WADAI, is one of the last of the German Africa Lines' passenger liners still afloat.

WADAI   4 696 grt   **WAHEHE**   4 709 grt
110m x 15,2m
Passengers carried in three classes.
Built: Reihersteig Schiffsw., Hamburg, 1922.
Quadruple expansion engines, oil burning, single screw, 11 knots.

Three very popular vessels on the South African coast between the wars, they provided many South Africans with holidays afloat. They were steady and comfortable vessels and provided good value for money. Not one of these vessels survived World War II.

The ADOLPH WOERMANN was in Mombasa when the war clouds started to gather and she took on board a number of passengers: Germans wanting to get home before the war started. She left Mombasa shortly before war was declared and made a wide sweep around the Cape in an effort to get to Germany. However, on 29 November 1939, she was stopped by the British cruiser, HMS NEPTUNE, in the South Atlantic. Her crew scuttled the vessel to avoid her being captured.

The USAMBARA was in Germany when the war started and was used as an accommodation vessel. She was in Stettin on 25 March 1945, when, during an air raid on that port, she was hit several times and reduced to a wreck. She was probably dismantled after the war.

The NJASSA was also in Germany at the outbreak of war and was also taken up as an accommodation vessel. She was found after the war, badly damaged and beyond repair, and so was broken up for scrap. They were beautiful small liners, with airy accommodation ideally suited for tropical cruising. They deserved better ends.

USAMBARA

ADOLPH WOERMANN   8 577 grt
USAMBARA   8 690 grt   **NJASSA**   8 754 grt
132,3m x 17,7m (Usambara 17,1m)
Passengers carried in three classes.
Built: Blohm and Voss, Hamburg, 1922, 1924, 1922.
Four steam turbines, single screw, 14 knots.

TANGANJIKA

TANGANJIKA   8 540 grt   136,9m x 17,8m
Passengers carried in three classes.
Built: Blohm and Voss, Hamburg, 1922.
Four steam turbines, single screw, 14 knots.

Though similar in appearance to the ADOLPH WOERMANN class, the TANGANJIKA was, in fact, a different class of vessel. She was more than four metres longer and had different arrangements. Like all German liners on the South African run, she was a popular vessel, particularly with coastal tourists, though many preferred to travel overseas in them rather than by the mail passenger service. The TANGANJIKA was in Germany when World War II broke out, and was used as an accommodation vessel at Wilhelmshaven where she was sunk during an air raid on the port in 1943. After the war, she was raised and broken up.

The UBENA was built to German East Africa Line account, and the WATUSSI for the Woermann Line, and both soon became very popular vessels on the South African trade. For some reason, the WATUSSI was always the more popular of the two, though there was little to choose between the standard of accommodation in the two vessels.

The WATUSSI had cleared Durban shortly before World War II started, and made for Maputo for shelter. She remained in Mozambique's territorial waters for some time, but, after having been painted in Union Castle colours and given a false name, she tried to round the Cape and make a dash for Germany. Early in December 1939, a patrolling aircraft of the South African Air Force found her about 100 miles south of Cape Point and ordered her to make for Simonstown. Soon clouds of smoke started to rise from her midships accommodation, and by the time a British cruiser arrived on the scene, the WATUSSI was well alight and settling fast. Her passengers and crew were rescued and spent the war in internment camps in South Africa.

The UBENA was more fortunate. She was in Germany when the war began and, like so many other German liners, was taken over for use as an accommodation vessel for the German Navy. After the war she was found in good condition and was awarded to Britain. She was renamed EMPIRE KEN and commissioned as a troop transport, owned by the Ministry of Transport and managed by the Royal Mail Lines. She was seen at Table Bay during the 1956 Suez crisis, her only visit after the war to her old haunts. She was broken up shortly afterwards.

WATUSSI

UBENA   9 523 grt   WATUSSI   9 521 grt
142,9m x 18,4m
Passengers in three classes.
Built: Blohm and Voss, Hamburg, 1928.
Four steam turbines, single screw, 14 knots, later 16 knots.

WINDHUK

The largest passenger liners built for the German Africa service, these two vessels, in the short time they were on the run, made a high reputation for themselves for service, comfort and cuisine. Apart from their normal service, they operated short 'into the blue' cruises at long weekends, such as Easter.

Their wartime careers, like those of so many of their consorts were divergent and varied. The PRETORIA was in Germany when the war broke out and was used, like her consorts, as an accommodation vessel. She was found intact after the war and became the British troop transport EMPIRE DOON. The WINDHUK, abroad at the outbreak of war, took shelter in a Brazilian port where she was seized when Brazil entered the war. The Brazilians handed her over to the Americans who took her to the United States, re-engined her and put her to work in the United States Navy as the Navy Transport LE JEUNE. The EMPIRE DOON, meanwhile, had been handed to the Orient Line for management and, to bring her into line with that company's policy of ships' names, she was renamed EMPIRE ORWELL. She ran for the Ministry of Transport until about 1963 when she was sold to Blue Funnel Line who renamed her GUNUNG DJATI and put her on their pilgrim service from Indonesia to Mecca. In 1973 she was sent to Hong Kong for a complete refit which included re-engining. She is still in service.

The LE JEUNE, ex-WINDHUK, was put in reserve by the United States Navy in 1955, and was sold for demolition shortly afterwards. In her later days, the LE JEUNE had only one funnel, an arrangement which rather spoiled her profile.

PRETORIA 16 662 grt WINDHUK 16 662 grt

167m x 22,1m
Passengers carried in three classes.
Built: Blohm and Voss, Hamburg, 1936.
Six steam turbines, twin screw, 17,5 knots.

HOLLAND AFRICA LINE

The Holland Africa Line, a comparative newcomer to the South African passenger trade, started services through its various component companies in the 1920s. The company, under its present name, came into being in 1932, and operated the passenger vessels with the well-known '-fontein' names.

Though new on the run, the Holland Africa liners soon became firm favourites, and during the heyday of passenger liners in the 1930s rarely sailed with many empty berths.

Declining trade in the 1960s and 1970s caused the company to cease their passenger carrying operations, and only freighters with the orange-banded black funnel are now seen in South African ports.

MELISKERK

MELISKERK, ex-Cesario, ex-DADG 76　　　6 045 grt

136,9m x 17,7m

Passengers carried in one class only.

Built: Blohm and Voss, Hamburg, 1919.

Quadruple expansion engines, single screw, coal burning, 12 knots.

One of the Holland Africa Line's smaller passengers liners, the MELISKERK started life as a vessel built by Germany as part of World War I reparations for Great Britain. She was owned originally by the David SS Co. Ltd, who, by 1925, had sold the vessel to the forerunners of the Holland Africa Line.

She was a familiar vessel in South African ports before World War II and was operating off the South African coast when, in January 1943, she struck a rock and was beached near Port St Johns. She blew up during the night after she stranded. It is said that the captain had instructions to take a course close inshore to avoid U-boats known to be operating off the South African coast, and had taken his instructions too literally.

The MELISKERK was one of the last three-masted steamers to be seen in South African waters. While her passenger accommodation could hardly have been described as palatial, it was adequate and comfortable.

RANDFONTEIN

Built for the Norwegian firm of Fearnley and Eger as the STAUR, this vessel was bought by Holland Africa and put on the passenger service to South Africa. She was the first of their passenger liners to bear a '-FONTEIN' name.

She served the company until the outbreak of World War II, which she survived. She was renamed RANDKERK to make way for the new RANDFONTEIN, and was soon after sold for breaking up.

She carried 40 passengers in a single class of a comfortable though not luxurious standard.

RANDFONTEIN, ex-Staur   5 653 grt
124,7m x 16,4m
Passengers carried in one class only.
Built: Greenock Dockyard Co. Ltd., Greenock, 1920.
Triple expansion engines, single screw, 12 knots.

BOSCHFONTEIN

BOSCHFONTEIN, ex-Nieuwkerk   7 139 grt

144m x 18,1m

Passengers originally in one class, later in two classes.

Built: NV Mch. and Schpsw. Maats P. Smit, Rotterdam, 1928.

Deschelde diesels, single screw, 14 knots.

Built as the NIEUWKERK, she was taken in hand in 1934 and was almost completely rebuilt. Her length, originally 125,1 metres, was added to by the fitting of new bows so that she came out 144 metres long overall. Her passenger accommodation was redesigned so that she carried passengers in two classes. She was one of the first vessels seen in South African waters with a maierform bow, something that looked unattractive, but was said to improve the sea-keeping qualities of the vessel.

The BOSCHFONTEIN came out under that name in 1934 after her refit. She was joined by two new vessels of similar appearance but much large dimensions.

After giving valuable service during World War II, the BOSCHFONTEIN returned to her peacetime role until the advent of newer vessels in the 1950s. She was then put on a service from Holland to Beira via the Suez Canal. Later she was reduced to a cargo-only vessel and renamed BOSCHKERK. She was later disposed of for scrap.

These two vessels were the first to be specifically built for the Holland Africa Line's service to South Africa and were given typically South African names. The BLOEMFONTEIN was launched by Mrs J.B.M. Hertzog, wife of the then prime minister of South Africa, by radio from her home in Bloemfontein.

The contrast between the standard of accommodation in the first class and that in the tourist class in these liners was very marked. The latter was confined almost entirely to the poop deck and after part of the vessel, while the first class had the run of the centre superstructure. They differed from other passenger liners in that they carried more first class than tourist class passengers. This was a characteristic of Holland Africa vessels until their last liner, the RANDFONTEIN, which came out in 1958.

Both the BLOEMFONTEIN and JAGERSFONTEIN gave sterling service during World War II, one of them being the first Allied vessel to assist the American forces after — in fact during — the attack on Pearl Harbour.

The JAGERSFONTEIN was torpedoed by U 107 on 26 June 1942 when 500 miles east of Bermuda, while on a voyage from Galveston, Texas, to Liverpool. There was no loss of life.

The BLOEMFONTEIN survived the war and returned to her normal service soon after the return of peace. She continued in the service until 1959 when she was sold to Hong Kong shipbreakers.

BLOEMFONTEIN

BLOEMFONTEIN	10 081 grt	
JAGERSFONTEIN	10 083 grt	148,8m x 19,3m

Passengers carried in two classes.
Built: NV Nederland Schps. Maats, Amsterdam, 1934.
Stork diesels, twin screws, 16 knots.

JAGERSFONTEIN

JAGERSFONTEIN	10 574 grt	160,9m x 19,2m
KLIPFONTEIN	10 544 grt	158,5m x 19,2m
ORANJEFONTEIN	10 549 grt	160,7m x 19,2m

Passengers carried in two classes.
Built: J'ftn — F. Schichaur, Danzig, launched 1940, completed 1950.
K'ftn — O'ftn — NV Mch. and Schps. van P. Smit, Rotterdam, 1939, 1940.
Diesel engines, twin screw, 17 knots.

These three liners were intended as sisters, but the war intervened, and they did not appear together until 1950. The KLIPFONTEIN was first completed and was in service when World War II broke out. She had completed only a few voyages when she was requisitioned for war service. The ORANJEFONTEIN was completing when Holland was overrun in 1940 and the vessel was taken by the German Navy to Kiel where she was used as a floating barracks until recovered after the war. The JAGERSFONTEIN, though, had the most chequered career of the three.

She was laid down as the RIETFONTEIN but was launched as the ELANDSFONTEIN. She was being built by the Danzig shipyard as part payment for tobacco supplied to Germany by Holland. After the German invasion of Holland, work on the liner stopped for a while, and later in the war she was severely damaged by bombing. She was found on her side in Danzig after the Russians took the city, and they had intentions of raising her and taking her to Russia. It took a considerable amount of diplomatic activity to get the Russians to release the vessel, but eventually she was returned to her Dutch owners. She was completed in Holland and renamed JAGERSFONTEIN to commemorate the vessel torpedoed in 1942. She joined the fleet in 1950.

The KLIPFONTEIN, while on a voyage up the east coast of Africa, struck a submerged object on 8 January 1953, and sank. There was no loss of life and all survivors were taken on board the Union Castle liner BLOEMFONTEIN CASTLE. Her cargo of copper attracted salvage divers for some time afterwards.

The JAGERSFONTEIN and ORANJEFONTEIN, later joined by the new RANDFONTEIN, carried on in the service until 1967, when the depressed state of the passenger carrying trade forced their withdrawal. They were strictly speaking now 27 years old, though neither had been in commercial service for more than 17 years, so it was not surprising that no buyers could be found to take them for further trading, and they ended their careers in the shipbreakers yards.

They had been popular vessels, and their coastal voyages from Table Bay or Durban to Beira and back were much sought after. Their first class accommodation was of a very high standard, and, as was to be expected of Dutch ships, their cheese board was superb. Their tourist class accommodation was very much advanced on that of the pre-war vessels.

RANDFONTEIN

The RANDFONTEIN came out as a replacement for both the BOSCHFONTEIN, which had been taken out of the passenger service, and the KLIPFONTEIN, which had been wrecked. She was the largest liner built for Holland Africa; she was also the last.

The RANDFONTEIN was unique among Holland Africa passenger liners. She was the only liner in the company in which tourist class passengers could outnumber those in the first class.

In 1971, with the changing trade patterns, the RAND-FONTEIN was sold to the Royal Interocean Lines who re-named her NIEUW HOLLAND, and put her into their service between Australia and Hong Kong and ports in Japan. This arrangement, however, did not prove successful and she was withdrawn from service in 1974 and offered for sale. She was bought by anonymous Far Eastern buyers, and is now a unit in the merchant fleet of Communist China.

RANDFONTEIN   13 694 grt   178m x 21,3m
Passengers carried in two classes.
Built: Wilton-Fijenoord, Schiedam, 1958.
Diesels, twin screw, 18 knots.

62

LLOYD TRIESTINO LINE

The Italian shipping company Navigazione Libera Triestina began a round-Africa service down the east coast and home by the west coast in 1925. Five years later a service taking the reverse route was started. During the 1930s the company came under the houseflag of the Lloyd Triestino Line which took over the services. World War II interrupted the services but they were restarted in 1948 and continued until early 1976 when the EUROPA took the last of the Lloyd Triestino passenger sailings.

Extremely popular vessels with a high standard of catering, the ships of the Lloyd Triestino had become household names in their short time in the South African passenger trade. Now only the occasional freighter is seen in South African ports to remind one of the glory that was once Rome — or, rather, Lloyd Triestino.

MAIELLA

MAIELLA, ex-Ambra   5 524 grt

121,9m x 16,5m

Passengers carried in one class only.

Built: Cantiere Nav. Triestino, Montafalcone, 1913.

Triple expansion engines, single screw, coal burning, 10 knots.

PERLA   5 741 grt   **SABBIA**   5 788 grt

118,9m x 16,5m

Passengers carried in one class only.

Built: Clyde Shipbuilding and Engineering Co. Ltd., Port Glasgow, 1926.

Triple expansion engines, single screw, coal burning, 11 knots.

SISTIANA, ex-Salvore   5 827 grt

118,9 m x 16,5m

Passengers carried in one class only.

Built: Stabilimento Tecnico Triestino, Trieste, 1924.

Triple expansion engines, single screw, coal burning, 11 knots.

The Navigazione Libera Triestina company started their round-Africa service with these four vessels in 1925. All the vessels took on the Lloyd Triestino houseflag when they came under that company in the early 1930s.

They were unspectacular and unostentatious vessels, but they found favour with many travellers. They provided comfortable quarters, good cuisine, and a restful voyage to or from South Africa.

World War II was unkind to these vessels, none of which survived the hostilities. The MAIELLA, which had been sold out of the fleet in 1939 to Giuseppe Gavarone and renamed NINETTO G, was torpedoed and sunk by a British submarine in the Straits of Messina on 5 April 1942, while on war service.

The PERLA, which had been taken over by the Italian government as a transport, was sunk three months earlier, on 7 January 1942, by British aircraft when south of Pantellaria on a voyage to North Africa.

No record can be found of the fate of the SABBIA, but it is presumed she was lost during the war as her name disappears completely from the shipping registers after the war.

The SISTIANA had a more varied career. She was taken prize when Italy entered World War II and was taken into the fleet of the British Ministry of War Transport. At first she was renamed MYRICA, but the following year, in accordance with the practice of giving captured enemy vessels names with the prefix EMPIRE, she was renamed EMPIRE UNION. She was registered in Glasgow, and was put under the management of the Canadian Pacific Steamship Company.

While on a voyage from London to St John, New Brunswick, at 11h40 on Boxing Day, 1942, she was torpedoed and sunk by a U-boat. Her captain, five of the crew and one of the DEMS gunners went down with the ship.

They were not very good-looking vessels, they were not fast and they did not catch the imagination of the public in the manner in which later vessels did, but they did pioneer a service which lasted for 50 years and reached the height of popularity. They served their company well.

LEME

LEME   8 124 grt   142,5m x 17,4m
Passengers carried in one class only.
Built: Stabilimento Tecnico Triestino, Trieste, 1925.
Diesel engines, twin screw, 14 knots.

The LEME was brought on the round-Africa service of Navigazione Libera Triestina in 1932 and remained on that service after the company came under the umbrella of the Lloyd Triestino a year or so later. She was a regular, if unostentatious visitor to South African ports until Italy entered World War II in June, 1940.

Shortly after Italy's entry into the war, the LEME was captured and declared prize of war. The following year she was renamed LOWLANDER, an exception to the EMPIRE nomenclature for captured enemy vessels, was registered in London and was put under the management of the Port Line. She remained under that management for the rest of the war and for a short while afterwards, during which time she visited Cape Town and Durban several times. Her tonnage was reduced to 8 059 gross registered tons.

In 1948 the Ministry of War Transport sold the vessel to the Italia Line of Genoa, and she reverted to her original name. The price paid was said to have been 'nominal'. Her new owners registered her in Genoa and her tonnage was again reduced, this time to 8 039 gross registered tons.

She served the Italia Line until about 1962 when she was disposed of for scrap, being then more than 35 years old, a good age for a motor vessel of her era.

The LEME did not return to the South African service after her sale to the Italia Line.

66

Owned by Navigazione Libera Triestina, these vessels came under the Lloyd Triestino house flag during the 1930s. They had been running in the South African service for some years before that, and their change of house flag made little or no difference to their routine. Not of an attractive appearance, they were three-island vessels with four masts, an unusual arrangement for ships in that period. Their passenger accommodation was comfortable without being lavish, but as they were the only direct sea link with Italy at that time, they were usually assured of a full complement.

The DUCHESSA D'AOSTA was taken over by the Allies in 1943 and was renamed EMPIRE YUKON. After the war she was sold to the Petrinovic Steamship Company who renamed her PETCONNIE, registered in Glasgow. Sold back to Italian owners in 1953 and renamed LIU O, she served until the end of the 1950s when she was disposed of for scrap.

The TIMAVO left Durban hours before Italy declared war in 1940, and was pursued up the coast by the South African Air Force. Rather than surrender his vessel, the captain ran her aground on the coast of Zululand. Her cargo was later salvaged but the TIMAVO became a total wreck and soon broke up.

The ROSANDRA became prominent in the early 1930s when she grounded south of Walvis Bay and provided Cape Town tugs with a long towage haul. She was torpedoed and sunk by a British submarine off the coast of Albania on 15 June 1943.

The fate of the PIAVE is not known, but it is presumed that she became a war loss during the Mediterranean campaigns.

PIAVE

DUCHESSA D'AOSTA		7 872 grt	
PIAVE	7 565 grt	ROSANDRA	8 034 grt
TIMAVO	7 549 grt	141,5m x 17,5m	

Passengers carried in one class only.
Built: D. d'Aosta — Stabilimento Tecnico Triestino, Trieste, 1921.
Others — Cantiere San Rocco, Trieste, 1921, 1921, 1920.
Triple expansion engines, coal burning, converted for oil 1930, single screw, 12 knots.

GERUSALLEME

GERUSALEMME, ex-Cracovia   8 052 grt   135,2m x 16,2m
Passengers carried in two classes.
Built: Cantiere San Rocco, Trieste, 1920.
Four steam turbines, twin screw, 13,5 knots.

A popular little liner before World War II, the war caught her in Maputo in 1940 and she remained at anchor there until after the Italian armistice in 1943. She was then taken over by the Allies and used as a hospital ship until the end of the war. She was returned to her owners after the war and, after a refit, was returned to the Lloyd Triestino passenger service from Italy to Durban through the Suez Canal.

The GERUSALEMME was withdrawn and sold for breaking up in 1952 after new tonnage had come into service.

She was nicely proportioned and the placing of her single funnel and twin masts gave her a pleasing profile. Her accommodation was above average for the period, and her service and cuisine set a standard which other Italian vessels were to follow and improve upon in later years.

When these two vessels, which, despite their apparent difference in size, were sisterships, came onto the Italy to South Africa run in 1933, there was more than a flutter in the dovecotes of the mail passenger company. They were three knots faster than anything the Union Castle line then owned, and since they had secured a contract with the South African government to carry mails to Italy, were seen as a potential threat to the well-being of the English mail contract. However, the Lloyd Triestino contract lapsed in 1938 and both vessels were withdrawn from service. They had left their mark, however, and the Union Castle Company had by that time brought out two new vessels of equal speed and had another on the stocks. Five others were being re-engined.

Very little of this behind-the-scenes activity was evident to the ordinary sea traveller who saw the two vessels, not as a threat to the mail contract, but as an introduction to *la dolce vita* (the good life), which the successors to the DUILIO and GIULIO CESARE were to provide in good measure after the war.

During their short service of five years on the South African run, the two vessels earned a reputation for regularity, comfort and luxury never before experienced by South African ocean travellers. During the war the DUILIO was used as a hospital ship by the Italian government. Taken over by the German forces after the Italian surrender, she was moved north. She was bombed and sunk by Allied aircraft in Trieste on 10 November 1944. After the war her hulk was raised and broken up.

The GIULIO CESARE suffered a similar fate, being sunk by bombs in September 1944. Her hulk was broken up in 1947.

GIULIO CESARE

DUILIO 23 635 grt   **GIULIO CESARE** 21 900 grt
193,7m x 23,3m and 193,2m x 23,2m respectively
Passengers carried in three classes.
Built: G. Cesare — Swan Hunter and Wigham Richardson, Newcastle, 1921.
Duilio — S.A. Ansaldo, Sestri, Ponente, 1923.
Four steam turbines, quadruple screw, 19 knots.

TOSCANA

TOSCANA, ex-Saarbrucken   9 584 grt   146,2m x 17,5m
Passengers carried in three classes, later one class only.
Built: AG 'Weser', Bremen, 1923.
Triple expansion engines, twin screw, 12 knots.

Built as the SAARBRUCKEN for the Nord Deutsche Lloyd, this vessel was bought by Lloyd Triestino and used on their service from Italy to Colombo and Australia, via the Suez Canal.

She was not seized as reparations after the war and remained in the ownership of Lloyd Triestino who used her to re-open their Africa service. She arrived in Durban on 7 January 1948, the first Italian vessel seen in that port since the TIMAVO had left on the eve of war in 1940.

She was later transferred to the company's service to South America, and was withdrawn and laid up in 1960. As no buyers came forward to take her for further trading, she was sold and broken up for scrap in 1962.

Within her limited capabilities, she did much to restore the Lloyd Triestino reputation for comfortable and luxurious travel during the few years she was on the Africa service.

70

These were the first passenger liners built by Lloyd Triestino for their service to South Africa after the war. They maintained and improved on the standard that had been set by the DUILIO and GIULIO CESARE before World War II, and soon became very popular liners. From Cape Town, the two vessels were able to provide coastal cruises between that port and Durban. They were also popular for their cruises on the east coast of Africa, when their terminal port was Beira. As the troubles in Mozambique increased, the two vessels turned at Maputo, and later went no further than Durban.

The two vessels were withdrawn from service in late 1975 and early 1976 respectively, the price of fuel, oil and other necessities for the maintenance of the service having made it uneconomical. Both were laid up in Italy.

In late 1976 the EUROPA was sold to Ahmed Mohamed Baaboud of Jedda to be used as a pilgrim ship between the East Indies and Mecca. She was renamed BLUE SEA, but before she was able to make her first voyage under new ownership she caught fire and was burned out. She became a constructive total loss.

The AFRICA was also sold and has been renamed PROTEA. Nothing more is known of her new role.

EUROPA

AFRICA   11 427 grt   EUROPA   11 430 grt
159,3m x 20,8m
Passengers carried in two classes.
Built: Africa – Cantieri Riunitti dell Monfalcone, 1952.
Europa – Ansaldo, Spezia, 1952.
Fiat diesels, twin screw, 19,5 knots.

NATAL LINE

Bullard, King and Company was one of the oldest shipping companies serving South Africa. It was founded in the 1850s to provide a direct service between the United Kingdom and Natal, and was known as the Natal Direct Line, meaning that its vessels did not stop at the Cape. Their first steamer came out in 1879.

In later years the company came under the control of the Union-Castle Company and when that company was absorbed by the Clan Line, the Natal Line followed. Shortly afterwards the company was wound up, its vessels going into the newly-formed Springbok Line. That company was very soon taken over by the South African Marine Corporation and the old Natal Line disappeared altogether.

Built as 'Extra' steamers for the Union Castle Company, when they carried passengers in three classes, these two vessels were transferred to Bullard, King's Natal Line in 1924. Their passenger accommodation was radically modified and reduced, and they soon became very popular with the South African travelling public because of the comfort they offered at what was even then a very reasonable rate.

Because they were manned by lascar crews, neither vessel was affected by the great shipping strike in 1925 and they were among the few vessels which were able to 'carry on as usual'. The UMVOTI was actually pressed into service as a mail steamer, carrying the Royal Mail in August 1925, when she left Table Bay with every berth occupied.

The UMKUZI was sold in 1938 and dismantled the same year. The UMVOTI carried on for a little longer, and was due to come out of service in 1939 when World War II broke out. She was bought by the British government in 1940 and used, together with a number of other out-dated vessels, to form an additional breakwater at Folkestone harbour. In 1943 she was raised and broken up at Ward's Folkestone shipbreaking yard. The UMVOTI's end was a most unusual one for a Cape liner.

UMVOTI

UMKUZI, ex-Cluny Castle   5 175 grt
UMVOTI, ex-Comrie Castle   5 183 grt   127,8m x 15,3m
Passengers carried in one class only.
Built: Barclay, Curle and Co., Glasgow, 1903.
Triple expansion engines, coal burning, twin screw, 12,5 knots.

UMONA

UMONA   3 767 grt   108,5m x 13,6m
Passengers carried in one class only.
Built: Sir J. Laing and Sons, Sunderland, 1910.
Triple expansion engines, coal burning, single screw, 12 knots.

The UMONA was the type of small passenger liner that used to call at South African ports so quietly that only her agents, passengers and crew might know she had been and gone. For all that she was well-liked among the travelling public before and after World War I. During that war she had a varied career, first serving as a collier for the Russian government and later as an auxiliary vessel for the Royal Naval Air Service. The last years she spent as a government collier in United Kingdom waters.

Her career in the second war in which she was involved was not as long, but more violent. She was torpedoed and sunk south west of Freetown on 30 March 1941, by a German U-boat. Two gunners, 15 passengers and 83 of her crew were lost. There were only three survivors from the disaster.

UMVUMA

The UMVUMA was the last vessel built for Bullard, King and Company before the Natal Line was bought by Lord Kylsant. She was completed in December 1914, and did not commence commercial service until 1919. During the later years of World War I she was used as a collier and ammunition carrier in the North Russian campaign against the Bolsheviks.

Like her consorts, she became very popular on the South African coast, the route she plied without serious incident until World War II broke out in 1939. She was almost immediately taken up by the Ministry of War Transport. She met her end as she had begun life — during wartime. She was 10 miles south of Mauritius, at the end of a voyage from London to Port Louis and within sight of her destination, when on 8 August 1943, she was torpedoed and sunk by a German submarine with the loss of one gunner, four of her passengers and 17 of her crew.

UMVUMA   4 419 grt   111,2m x 15m
Passengers carried in one class only.
Built: Sir J. Laing and Sons, Sunderland, 1914.
Triple expansion engines, coal burning, single screw, 13 knots.

UMGENI

UMTATA	8 141 grt	UMTALI	8 162 grt
UMGENI	8 180 grt	137,6m x 18,7m	

Passengers carried in one class only.
Built: Swan Hunter and Wigham Richardson, Newcastle, 1935, 1936, 1938.
Triple expansion engines, coal burning, twin screw, 14 knots.

The largest and last passenger liners built for the Natal Line, these vessels were firm favourites among sea travellers to and from South Africa. Each carried more than 100 passengers in a style and comfort which was already, in the 1930s, beginning to disappear from the oceans of the world. Their accommodation was well designed, comfortable but unostentatious. The service given by the Goanese and lascar stewards was the company's best advertisement.

All three were taken up for war service when World War II started. The UMGENI and UMTALI survived the war with high reputations for services rendered; the UMTATA, unfortunately, was torpedoed and sunk off the coast of Florida on 7 July 1942, without loss of life.

The two survivors, with a new UMTALI, which carried only 12 passengers, revived the company's service shortly after the end of the war. The demand for sea passages, however, had declined, and shortly after the company had been absorbed by the new British and Commonwealth shipping group in 1957, the two passenger liners were sold to Elder Dempster Ltd., who renamed them WINNEBA (ex-UMGENI) and CALABAR (ex-UMTALI). They were put on their new owners' West African service. They had a few years of service left before the CALABAR went to Inverkeithing for breaking up in January 1963, and the WINNEBA to a Belgian shipbreaker in March of the same year. The affairs of Bullard, King and Company were wound up shortly after the vessels were sold to Elder Dempster, and another longstanding service came to an end.

THE NETHERLANDS GOVERNMENT

This service, operated by three vessels belonging to the government of the Netherlands, was the only government operated passenger liner service ever to be seen in South African waters. Its main purpose was to provide transport for the many Hollanders then wishing to emigrate to South Africa. The vessels took about six sailings each year and called only at Walvis Bay and Cape Town. They carried about 830 passengers on the outward voyage, and accepted passengers on the homeward voyage at very competitive fares. Later, the Dutch government used these vessels on other routes for similar purposes. The service came to an end in the early 1960s when the migrant trade declined, and the vessels were sold.

ZUIDERKRUIS

These three vessels were unusual among liners calling at Table Bay in that they were owned by the Netherlands government and were used specifically to carry emigrants from that country to the lands of their choice overseas.

They were built as 'Victory' ships in the United States and were among a number that were fitted as troop transports. This, however, did not hide the distinctive lines of their hulls, and their origins were obvious to all. These three were taken over by the Netherlands government in 1947 and converted for carrying passengers by shipyards in Holland. Their accommodation was comfortable but not luxurious, and they could carry about 1000 passengers on each voyage.

During the 1950s they were seen frequently in Table Bay, their terminal port in South Africa. On their return voyages, they offered passages at very low rates; the travelling public were not slow to take full advantage of this.

They were used on other routes occasionally, but were used mainly on the run to South Africa. In the early 1960s, when the migrant trade declined, the Dutch government disposed of them. The GROOTE BEER and WATERMAN were sold to John S. Latsis of Piraeus, Greece, who put them into service out of Piraeus; the ZUIDERKRUIS was transferred to the Royal Netherlands Navy for use as a stores and accommodation vessel. She was broken up in Bilbao, Spain, in 1969.

GROOTE BEER, ex- Costa Rica Victory   9 140 grt
WATERMAN, ex-La Grande Victory   9 177 grt
ZUIDERKRUIS, ex-Cranston Victory   9 178 grt
138,8m x 19m
Passengers carried in emigrant accommodation.
Built: Groote Beer — Permanente Shipyard No. 1, Richmond, 1944.
Others — Oregon Shipbuilding Corp., Portland, 1945, 1944.
Two steam turbines, single screw, 17 knots.

OSAKA SHOSEN KAISHA

An old-established Japanese shipping company, the Osaka Shosen Kaisha sent their first vessel to South Africa in 1917. Their first passenger sailings were in 1925, and in 1931 they took over the service up till then operated by the Nippon Yusen Kaisha. The itinerary of the OSK liners was very interesting. Leaving Japan, they called at Hong Kong, Saigon, Singapore, Colombo, Durban, Port Elizabeth, Cape Town, Rio de Janeiro and other South American ports, New Orleans and Galveston in the United States, and then home to Japan through the Panama Canal.

A second service took in the same Far East stops, then on to the various ports of East Africa with Durban as the terminal port. Later this service was extended so that the turn-round took place in South America.

Most of the OSK liners were lost during World War II, and, apart from two or three once-only visits by OSK passenger liners, the company's passenger services to South Africa and South America were not revived after World War II. Their freighters, now operating under the flag of Mitsui-OSK, are frequent visitors to South African ports.

HAWAII MARU

HAWAII MARU 9 467 grt   **MANILA MARU** 9 846 grt
144,8m x 18,6m
Passengers carried in one class and steerage.
Built: Hawaii Maru — Kawasaki Dockyard Co. Ltd., Kobe, 1915.
Manila Maru — Mitsubishi Dockyard and Engineering Works, Nagasaki, 1915.
Triple expansion engines, coal burning, converted for oil in 1924, twin screw, 12 knots.

These two liners were frequent visitors to South African ports during the 1930s while carrying Japanese emigrants to South America. They were fitted with comfortable accommodation for a limited number of passengers in cabins. The emigrants, however, occupied accommodation, the space for which was used for cargo on the return voyage.

Both vessels were lost during World War II. The MANILA MARU was torpedoed and sunk by the American submarine MINGO 120 miles west of Brunei, Borneo, on 25 November 1944. The HAWAII MARU was sunk by a torpedo from the American submarine SEA DEVIL 150 miles south west of Kagoshima, Japan, exactly one week later, on 2 December.

ARIZONA MARU

Like the HAWAII MARU class, these liners were brought onto the Japan to South America route via the Cape to cater for the large number of Japanese emigrating to South America during the 1930s. Their accommodation was very similar to the earlier class.

All three were lost during World War II. The AFRICA MARU was torpedoed by the American submarine FIN-BACK on 20 October 1942, while on a voyage through the Formosa Strait. The ARIZONA MARU was bombed and sunk by aircraft off the Solomon Islands the following month, on 14 November. The last of the trio, the ARABIA MARU, was torpedoed by the United States submarine BLUEGILL on 18 October 1944, about 100 miles east of Manila while serving as an Imperial Japanese Army transport.

AFRICA MARU 9 476 grt   **ARABIA MARU** 9 480 grt
ARIZONA MARU   9 684 grt
144,8m x 18,6m
Passengers carried in one class and steerage.
Built: Mitsubishi Soshen Kaisha, Nagasaki, 1918, 1918, 1920.
Triple expansion engines, coal burning, converted for oil in 1924, twin screw, 12 knots.

LA PLATA MARU

The SANTOS MARU was the first passenger liner that the Osaka Steamship Company put on the route from Japan to South America via South African ports. The other two vessels followed her the next year.

With limited first class accommodation, they had large dormitory accommodation fitted in the tween decks for the hundreds of Japanese emigrants which they carried each voyage to South America. The space was used for cargo on the voyage back to Japan. The MONTEVIDEO MARU became a war casualty when she was torpedoed and sunk west of Luzon Island in the Phillipines by the United States submarine STURGEON on 1 June 1942.

The fates of the other two vessels are somewhat shrouded in mystery. No record comes to light on what happened — or did not happen — to the LA PLATA MARU, while two authorities give different fates for the SANTOS MARU. One says that the vessel was torpedoed and sunk on 25 November 1944, some 50 miles south west of Basco in the Batan Islands, by the American submarine ATULE; the other says the vessel survived the war, was renamed MANZYU MARU and was put back into service by her pre-war owners. Perhaps it was the SANTOS MARU that was torpedoed, and that it was the LA PLATA MARU which was renamed.

Whatever happened to the SANTOS MARU and the LA PLATA MARU, neither vessel returned to the Osaka SK's pre-war passenger service to South America, which was not revived after the war. The company still runs passenger services, but none of their passenger liners calls at South African ports now.

LA PLATA MARU   MONTEVIDEO MARU
SANTOS MARU   7 267 grt   131,1m x 17,1m
Passengers carried in one class and steerage.
Built: Mitsubishi Shosen Kaisha, Nagasaki, 1926, 1926, 1925.
Sulzer diesels, twin screw, 14 knots.

82

BUENOS AIRES MARU

These two vessels formed the second class of vessel built especially for the OSK service between Japan and South America via South Africa. The emigrant accommodation in these vessels was much like that in earlier vessels, but the cabin passengers enjoyed greatly superior services.

They were good looking vessels for their time and were popular with the travelling public who wanted a quiet voyage to the Far East. The round trips from South African ports to South America and back were among the first of their kind offered.

Neither vessel survived World War II. The BUENOS AIRES MARU was bombed and sunk by aircraft off St Matthias Island on 27 November 1943, while the RIO DE JANEIRO MARU, which had been converted to a submarine tender by the Japanese Navy, was caught at Truk by American carrier-born aircraft, bombed and sunk.

BUENOS AIRES MARU   9 626 grt
RIO DE JANEIRO MARU   9 627 grt
140,6m x 18,9m
Passengers carried in one class and steerage.
Built: Mitsubishi Soshen Kaisha, Nagasaki, 1929, 1930.
Mitsubishi diesels, twin screw, 14 knots.

ARGENTINA MARU

The ARGENTINA MARU and BRASIL MARU were the largest and most luxurious passenger vessels put into service by the Osaka Shosen Kaisha on their Japan to South America via the Cape service. Both made their maiden voyages in 1939 before the start of World War II. The Japanese decor in the public rooms was the subject of much favourable comment when they arrived in Cape Town on their first voyages, and those South Africans who managed to make voyages in these vessels in the short time they were on the route were very impressed with the service and the standard of accommodation. The accommodation for the inevitable emigrants was also very superior to similar accommodation in earlier vessels. Both vessels remained on the South America run after the start of World War II.

Shortly after Pearl Harbour and Japan's entry into the war, the ARGENTINA MARU was taken over by the Japanese Navy and converted into an aircraft carrier. Her diesels were removed and a set of destroyer turbines were installed. This did not increase her speed as much as was intended and she spent most of her time as a training carrier and as an aircraft transport.

Before the BRASIL MARU could be converted similarly, she was sunk by the American submarine GREENLING on 5 August 1942, midway between Guam and Truk. She was carrying 400 soldiers, 200 passengers and a large crew at the time, and there was great loss of life.

The ARGENTINA MARU, which had been commissioned as the aircraft carrier KAIYO in November 1943, was bombed and sunk by aircraft in Beppu Bay, Kyushu, Japan, on 24 July 1945. She sank in shallow water and was later raised and dismantled.

OSK replaced both of these vessels after the war, but neither was a regular visitor to South African ports.

ARGENTINA MARU   12 755 grt   157,3m x 21m
BRASIL MARU   12 752 grt   165,8m x 21m

Passengers carried in first class and steerage.
Built: Mitsubishi Jukogyo Kaisha, Nagasaki, 1939.
Mitsubishi diesels, twin screw, 21 knots.

ROYAL INTEROCEAN LINES

In 1931, the Koninklijke Paketvaart Maatschappij, which was already firmly entrenched in the Far East passenger trade, started a regular passenger and cargo service between South Africa and the Dutch East Indies. They soon became popular on the South African seaboard, and before World War II had extended their operations beyond South Africa travellers to either the Far East or to South America.

After World War II, the KPM was amalgamated with the Java-China-Pacific Line to form the Royal Interocean Lines. Several of the latter company's vessels were put on the service which called at Singapore, the Philippines, Mauritius and several ports in South America.

The declining passenger trade eventually brought this service to an end in 1968 and the vessels were disposed of to shipbreakers or were put on other routes.

HOUTMAN

HOUTMAN   5 069 grt   119,4m x 15m
Passengers carried in one class only.
Built: Nedld. Schps. Maats., Amsterdam, 1913.
Triple expansion engines, single screw, 13 knots.

BARENTZ   4 819 grt   **ROGGEVEEN**   4 782 grt
116,5m x 14,8m
Passengers carried in one class only.
Built: Barentz – Nedld. Schps. Maats., Amsterdam, 1915.
Roggeveen – Maats. Fijenoord, Rotterdam, 1914.
Triple expansion engines, single screw, 13 knots.

TASMAN   4 992 grt   119,5m x 15m
Passengers carried in one class only.
Built: Earle's Co. Ltd., Hull, 1921.
Triple expansion engines, single screw, 13 knots.

These four vessels, all similar in appearance but not sister-ships, pioneered the KPM service from the Far East to South African ports in the early 1930s. Except for the BARENTZ, they were all regular visitors until the advent of the BOISSE-VAIN class shortly before World War II.

Comfortable and steady, they brought a touch of the East to South African ocean travel and soon became popular vessels, a reputation which their successors were to maintain. The vessels were taken off the service in 1938 and returned to the route among the islands of the Dutch East Indies. The HOUTMAN, though, was sent to the shipbreakers' yards.

TJISADANE

The TJISADANE was originally a unit of the Java-China-Japan Line and came on to old KPM route after the merger of the two companies after World War II. She was a typical Far East passenger trader, with airy accommodation and excellent service. A steady but unremarkable vessel, she was withdrawn from service in 1962 after 31 years of service in peace and war and was sold for demolition.

TJISADANE   9 228 grt   134,3m x 19m
Passengers carried in two classes.
Built: Nedld. Schps. Maats., Amsterdam, 1931.
Werkspoor diesels, single screw, 13 knots.

TJITJALENGKA

TJITJALENGKA   10 972 grt   138,6m x 19,7m
Passengers carried in two classes.
Built: Nedld. Schps. Maats., Amsterdam, 1939.
Stork diesels, single screw, 15 knots.

The TJITJALENGKA was completed shortly before World War II and was the largest vessel built for the Java-China-Japan Line, which has since been merged with the KPM to form the Royal Interocean Lines. After a short period in service in the Far East and Dutch East Indies, she was refitted as a hospital ship during the war. She served in this capacity until 1946 when she was returned to her owners.

The TJITJALENGKA plied the Far East route for some years before she was put on the service between the Far East, South Africa and South America. In 1962 she was reconditioned and air-conditioned, and returned to service for a further six years. In 1968, when the Royal Interocean Lines ceased passenger operations, she was taken out of service and sold for demolition.

RUYS

The largest triple screw motor vessels ever built, these three fine looking liners came into service between the Far East and South Africa in 1938. They provided first class accommodation and were very popular among the travelling public for their round trips to South America at very reasonable rates.

All three were used as troop transports during World War II, for which purpose they were ideally suited.

They were returned to their owners after the war and, after extensive refits, were put back into service. They now appeared in a different livery from that of pre-war years. They had been painted white all over and sported buff funnels; in their post-war guise they wore black paint on their hulls and their funnels were black with the house flag of the new company, Royal Interocean Lines, painted on them. This was hardly an improvement, but it would take more than black paint to hide the graceful lines of these three beautiful liners.

They ran in the service until the company ceased their passenger operations in 1968. All three disappeared into shipbreakers' yards soon afterwards.

BOISSEVAIN	14 134 grt	RUYS	14 155 grt
TEGELBERG	14 145 grt		

170,4m x 22m
Passengers carried in two classes.
Built: Boissevain — Blohm and Voss, Hamburg, 1937.
Ruys — NV Konink Maats., Flushing, 1937.
Tegelberg — Nedld. Schps. Maats., Amsterdam, 1937.
Sulzer diesels, triple screw, 16 knots.

STRAAT BANKA

STRAAT BANKA   9 161 grt
TJINEGARA, ex-Straat Makassar   9 067 grt
143,9m x 19,4m
Passengers carried in one class only.
Built: P. Smit Jnr. Rotterdam, 1952, 1951.
Diesel engines, single screw, 16 knots.

The last vessels to be built for the Far East to South Africa service with passenger accommodation, these two vessels boasted a very high standard of service. All the cabins had portholes and were all on one deck. The public rooms included a dining-room, lounge, writing room and library. There was also a shop, a hairdressing salon, and a permanent swimming pool. All this added up to an extremely high standard of accommodation for only 40 passengers.

Together with the older vessels in the fleet, the STRAAT BANKA and TJINEGARA operated the service until 1968 when the passenger operations of the fleet to South Africa and South America ceased. They were transferred to a new service from South Africa to Australia and New Zealand, but this did not prove successful, and the service was soon abandoned.

The two vessels were sold in 1971 to the Mercury Shipping Company and renamed MERCURY LAKE and MERCURY BAY respectively. They were used on a service between South African ports and the Persian Gulf. This service ceased in the middle of 1977 and the vessels were sold.

The TJINEGARA was originally named STRAAT MAKASSAR, but had her name changed in 1956 to commemorate a previous TJINEGARA which was lost by enemy action on 26 July 1942.

SHAW SAVILL AND ALBION LINE

This company was one of the oldest shipping concerns associated with the passenger trade to and from South Africa
with roots going back more than 100 years. In 1932 the
company acquired the remaining vessels of the Aberdeen-
White Star Line, which also had had very long associations
with South Africa.

Between the wars, the Shaw Savill and Albion Line ran
their service in conjunction with Alfred Holt's Blue Funnel
Line, but this arrangement lapsed at the outbreak of World
War II and was not revived.

The company ceased passenger carrying operations in
1975, and the cargo vessels of the company are rarely seen
in South African waters today.

THERMISTOCLES

THEMISTOCLES   11 231 grt

152,6m x 19m

Passengers carried in two classes, with temporary emigrant berths.

Built: Harland and Wolff Ltd., Belfast, 1911.

Quadruple expansion engines, coal burning, twin screw, 15 knots.

Built for George Thompson's Aberdeen Line, she was one of the vessels taken over by Shaw Savill and Albion when they bought the controlling interest in Aberdeen and Commonwealth Line in the early 1930s. She was retained in the fleet while her sister, the DEMOSTHENES, was sold for breaking up.

The THEMISTOCLES had been a troop transport in World War I and did good work during World War II. She was broken up at Dalmuir in 1947.

During her 36-year career, she was a steady plodding vessel, never fast enough to catch the public imagination, nor beautiful in a way to cause comment. She was remarkable only in that when she had left the service, her absence was noted.

In her later days she was painted in Shaw Savill and Albion livery, black hull, white superstructure and black-topped buff funnel; in her Aberdeen days she had sported a green hull, white upperworks and a plain buff funnel. She certainly looked better in the latter colour scheme.

Built originally for the White Star Line's Australia service, the CERAMIC was the biggest vessel calling at Cape Town until the advent of the ARUNDEL CASTLE in 1921. She was not exceeded in length until the arrival of the ATHLONE CASTLE in 1936.

When Shaw Savill and Albion took over the interests of the White Star Line's Australia service in the 1930s, the CERAMIC was one of the vessels that went with the deal. As the two companies had very similar livery, the change in ownership made very little difference to the old liner.

A troop transport in World War I, the CERAMIC was not taken up for war service in the second war, but remained on the run between the United Kingdom and Australia via the Cape. It was in this service that, on the night of 6 December 1942, she was torpedoed and sunk with great loss of life when off the Azores. Of the 378 passengers and 278 crew, only one man survived. He was taken prisoner by a U-boat the next day.

The submarine which sank the CERAMIC, the U 515, was later sunk by American destroyers; the captain, Kapt. Lt. W. Henke was subsequently shot while trying to escape from a prisoner of war camp.

CERAMIC

CERAMIC   18 713 grt   199,7m x 21,2m
Passengers carried in two classes, later in one class only.
Built: Harland and Wolff Ltd., Belfast, 1913.
Triple expansion engines and low power turbine, triple screw, 15 knots.

AKAROA

AKAROA, ex-Euripides   15 130 grt

167,8m x 20,5m

Passengers carried in two classes, later in one class only.

Built: Harland and Wolff Ltd., Belfast, 1914.

Triple expansion engines, triple screw, 15 knots.

One of the Aberdeen liners taken over by Shaw Savill and Albion in 1932, the AKAROA spent most of her time under this company's houseflag on the Australian run via the Panama Canal. Prior to that, though, she had been well known in Table Bay, so when she returned to South African waters as a temporary running mate to the DOMINION MONARCH after World War II, it was as if an old friend had returned.

She had served as a troop transport in World War I, and did similar service in World War II.

The AKAROA was withdrawn from service and sold for breaking up in 1954.

MATAROA

Two of the Aberdeen Line's vessels taken over in 1932, they were then taken off the run via the Cape and put into service on the route via the Panama Canal. However, they returned to the service via the Cape after World War II while four new vessels were being built. Both vessels were withdrawn from service and broken up at Faslane in Scotland in 1957.

MATAROA, ex-Diogenes   12 390 grt
TAMAROA, ex-Sophocles   12 405 grt
152,5m x 19,3m
Passengers carried in one class only.
Built: Harland and Wolff Ltd., Belfast, 1922.
Four steam turbines, twin screw, 15 knots.

ARAWA

ARAWA, ex-Esperance Bay 14 462 grt
ESPERANCE BAY, ex-Hobsons Bay 14 204 grt
JERVIS BAY 14 164 grt LARGS BAY 14 143 grt
MORETON BAY 14 145 grt
161,8m x 20,8m
Passengers carried in two classes, later in one class only.
Built: Arawa and Largs B. — Wm. Beardmore and Co. Ltd.,
Glasgow, 1922, 1921.
Others — Vickers Ltd., Barrow-on-Furness, 1922, 1922, 1921.
Four steam turbines, twin screw, 16 knots.

Built for the Australian government line and taken over by the Aberdeen Line to form the Aberdeen and Commonwealth Line, these five vessels were acquired by Shaw Savill and Albion in 1932. Originally on the route via the Cape, they were transferred to the Suez run. The JERVIS BAY was sunk as an armed merchant cruiser while defending a convoy in the North Atlantic on 5 November 1940. The other vessels, all except the MORETON BAY having been commissioned as auxiliary cruisers, survived the war. After refits, they were returned to service and all made regular calls at Table Bay or Durban between then and when they were sold for scrapping between 1955 and 1957.

The LARGS BAY was the first Shaw Savill and Albion liner to call at a South African port after the war.

The DOMINION MONARCH was the first quadruple screw motor liner seen in South African waters when she made her maiden voyage in the middle of 1939. That was to be her last peacetime voyage for almost eight years, as World War II had started before she returned to her home port at the end of her maiden voyage. She was immediately taken up for trooping and all the beautiful decorations and furniture were removed and put in store for the duration. As converted, she could carry 4 000 troops on each voyage. Her cargo space was retained and she was often, during the war, called on for special voyages which required the carriage of both troops and cargo.

She was released in July 1947, and resumed normal service in December 1948. She soon settled down on her run which took her to Australia via the Cape, returning the same way. Unlike other vessels in the fleet, she did not come out via the Cape and return via Panama.

In 1962 she was sold to Japanese shipbreakers, who hired her to the organizers of the World Fair at Seattle, Washington State, for use as a hotel ship. Scrapping eventually started at Osaka in November 1962.

Besides being the biggest quadruple screw vessel seen in South African waters, the DOMINION MONARCH was also the first large vessel seen with one mast, a fashion which was followed by most shipping companies after the war.

DOMINION MONARCH

DOMINION MONARCH   27 155 grt   207,9m x 25,8m
Passengers carried in one class only.
Built: Swan Hunter and Wigham Richardson, Newcastle, 1939.
Doxford diesels, quadruple screw, 19,5 knots.

GOTHIC

ATHENIC   15 187 grt   CERAMIC   15 896 grt
CORINTHIC   15 682 grt   GOTHIC   15 911 grt
170,8m x 21,9m

Passengers carried in one class only.

Built: A – Harland and Wolff Ltd., Belfast, 1947.

C/C – Cammell, Laird, and Co. Ltd., Birkenhead, 1948, 1947.

G – Swan Hunter and Wigham Richardson Ltd., Newcastle, 1948.

Six steam turbines, twin screw, 18 knots.

Four large cargo liners with spacious accommodation for 85 passengers, these vessels had uneventful careers in the main. The only one which came into the news was the GOTHIC which was twice fitted out as a royal yacht. She was so fitted in 1952 to carry Princess Elizabeth and the Duke of Edinburgh from Kenya to Australia and New Zealand. The death of King George VI caused this visit to be cancelled, and the vessel returned to her normal run. In 1954, however, she was taken up again for duty as a royal yacht, this time carrying the Queen and the Duke on their visit to the Antipodes.

The ATHENIC and CORINTHIC were reduced to cargo-only vessels in 1965, and the GOTHIC, after a serious fire at sea in 1968, went to the shipbreakers' yards in Taiwan. The ATHENIC and CORINTHIC followed shortly afterwards. The CERAMIC was the last to go when she went to Belgian shipbreakers in 1972.

SOUTHERN CROSS

This vessel, with her machinery sited aft and other revolutionary points to her design, caused a stir when she first appeared on the South African seaboard. Her accommodation also caused comment because of its high standard, particularly for a tourist class vessel. At first the SOUTHERN CROSS rarely sailed with empty berths. She seemed set for a long and successful career.

Slowly, though, over the 16 years during which Shaw Savill and Albion operated her, the number of vacant berths grew, until, by 1971, she became uneconomical to run. She went to the River Fal to be laid up, and there she lay for the next two years.

A new lease of life was given to her when Ulysses Lines bought her for cruising. She was given a thorough refit and her interior was redesigned. The psychedelic design which now graces the funnel is not an improvement, but some of the interior rooms have been improved during the refit. Now called CALYPSO, the vessel has been seen on cruise voyages in South African waters.

SOUTHERN CROSS   20 204 grt   182,9m x 23,8m
Passengers carried in tourist class only.
Built: Harland and Wolff Ltd., Belfast, 1955.
Four steam turbines, twin screw, 20 knots.

ARANDA

AKAROA, ex-Amazon   **ARAWA, ex-Aragon**
ARANDA ex-Arlanza   19 000 grt   178m x 23,8m
Passengers carried in one class only.
Built: Harland and Wolff Ltd., Belfast, 1959.
Diesel engines, twin screw, 17,5 knots.

These vessels were hardly on the run before they were off again. After nine years in the South American service of Royal Mail Lines, they were taken over by Shaw Savill and Albion and put in their round-the-world service in 1969. However, after three years, as the service proved to be unsuccessful, they were withdrawn and offered for sale.

The AKAROA went to A/S Uglands Rderi of Grimstad, Norway, and the other two went to Hoegh Lines. They were renamed AKARITA, HOEGH TRANSIT and HOEGH TRAVELLER respectively. They have been completely rebuilt as automobile carriers; in their new form they are unrecognizable as former Royal Mail or Shaw Savill liners. The two Hoegh vessels have passed through Table Bay since their conversion.

NORTHERN STAR

Following on the apparent success of the SOUTHERN CROSS, the company ordered a slightly larger version of the vessel with modifications thought necessary from experience in the SOUTHERN CROSS. It was intended that the two liners would run a round-the-world service together.

The NORTHERN STAR, however, was not a success. The migrant trade to Australia had dropped off, air travel was making greater and greater inroads into the tourist trade, and labour disputes added to the other troubles. A fire in her smoke room while she was in Durban in 1967, while not necessarily a contributory cause to her early demise, highlighted the unfortunate luck the ship had.

In 1975 the NORTHERN STAR was withdrawn from service and offered for sale. No buyer came forward to take her for further trading, and she went to the scrapyards, still a comparatively new vessel.

NORTHERN STAR   24 733 grt   181,3m x 25m
Passengers carried in one class only.
Built: Vickers Armstrong Ltd., Newcastle, 1962.
Steam turbines, twin screw, 22 knots.

SOUTH AFRICAN MARINE CORPORATION

The most recent entrant into the South African ocean passenger trade, Safmarine, as the company is best known, was also the only purely South African company engaged in that trade. Founded in 1947, the company was for many years engaged in the cargo trade, their vessels carrying no more than 12 passengers. In 1966 the company joined the Royal Mail service by buying two of the mail steamers from the Union-Castle Line, and for the past 11 years operated passenger liners.

With the departure of the SA VAAL in September 1977, a new era will be ushered in, that of the container vessel for which trade Safmarine has five such vessels in order.

The first mail passenger liner built by Union Castle Company after World War II, the SA ORANJE, was launched as the PRETORIA CASTLE by Mrs Issie Smuts, wife of Field Marshal J.C. Smuts, by radio from her home in Irene, Transvaal. She sailed under her first name until 2 February 1966, when she was renamed SA ORANJE by Mrs Betsie Verwoerd, wife of Dr H.F. Verwoerd, then prime minister of South Africa. The vessel had been transferred to the ownership of the South African Marine Corporation, though still to be manned and operated by Union Castle Company.

Like her sister, the EDINBURGH CASTLE, the SA ORANJE had a trouble-free career, missing only one voyage while she was being modernized. Towards the end of her career, the passenger trade fell off badly, and when it was decided to withdraw her from service because of age, it was decided not to replace her with another passenger liner. She was taken out of service in 1975, making her last voyage from Cape Town to Durban in October that year. She was destored in Durban, and from there sailed for Kaiosiung, Taiwan.

In her departure, the SA ORANJE chalked up an unusual distinction for herself. She was the first passenger vessel in the Union Castle fleet ever to complete her career without ever having taken part in any war or other national emergency.

SA ORANJE

SA ORANJE, ex-Pretoria Castle   28 705 grt
227,8m x 25,6m
Passengers carried in two classes.
Built: Harland and Wolff Ltd., Belfast, 1948.
Six steam turbines, twin screw, 22 knots.

SA VAAL as Transvaal Castle

SA VAAL,
ex-Transvaal Castle   30 212 grt   231,7m x 27,5m
Passengers in one class only.
Built: John Brown and Co. (Clydebank) Ltd., Glasgow, 1961.
Four steam turbines, twin screw, 22 knots.

The SA VAAL, when she came out in 1961 as the TRANS-VAAL CASTLE, was unique among the passenger mail liners. She was the only such liner designed to carry passengers in one class only, a class designated as hotel class. In effect, she carried the normal de luxe, first class and cabin class accommodation, the difference being that all passengers had the run of the ship and public rooms, and swimming baths and other amenities were open to all.

Though not the first passenger liner to be entered on the South African register of shipping, she was the largest. She was also the first mail steamer to be registered in a South African port. On 1 April 1976, she inaugurated the new harbour at Richards Bay, the first new harbour to be opened on the South African seaboard since Union in 1910.

Shortly before she left Table Bay for the last time in September 1977, it was announced that she had been sold to a London-based company of the customarily undisclosed nationality, to be used for cruising in the Caribbean, her new name to be FESTIVALE.

UNION-CASTLE LINE

The oldest shipping company with associations with South Africa, the Union-Castle Line goes back to 1853 when the Southampton Steam Collier Company was formed to provide coal for the then mail steamers of the General Screw Steam Shipping Company, the first company to run a regular mail service to the Cape. Four years later the collier company, renamed the Union Steamship Company, took over the mail contract and sent out its first vessel, the DANE. In 1872, Donald Currie sent out his first Castle liner, and in 1900 the two companies were amalgamated to form the Union-Castle Mail Steamship Company. This company became the main, and to many the only, passenger shipping company connecting South Africa with countries across the oceans.

In 1957 the Union-Castle Line was taken over by the Clan Line, and has steadily declined in size. Twenty years ago, the fleet comprised more than 14 passenger liners and a large number of refrigerated and dry cargo vessels; today, with the departure of the WINDSOR CASTLE, the last of the company's passenger liners, the fleet numbers only the GOOD HOPE CASTLE, the SOUTHAMPTON CASTLE and four freighters, ex-Clan Liners, which have been given Union-Castle names and livery.

ARMADALE CASTLE

These two vessels were the first mail steamers ordered by the new Union Castle Mail Steamship Company after the amalgamation in 1900. In 1904, on her third voyage, the ARMADALE CASTLE was the first mail steamer to cross the bar at Durban officially. When World War I broke out, the ARMADALE CASTLE was commissioned as an armed merchant cruiser, in which role she took part in the invasion of South West Africa, carrying General Louis Botha and later Lord Buxton, the Governor General of the Union, to Walvis Bay. Later she was a unit of the 10th Cruiser Squadron engaged on the northern blockade of Germany. She returned to normal service, after a refit, in 1919 and remained in the mail service until she was withdrawn in 1935, and was sold for scrap in the following year.

The KENILWORTH CASTLE was not taken up for war service until quite late in the war. She was one of the convoy of six vessels which took the last Imperial garrison from South Africa to the United Kingdom in August 1914, returning to the regular mail service early the following year. In June 1918 she was nearly lost following a collision with an escorting destroyer, HMS RIVAL. The KENILWORTH CASTLE sliced off the stern of the destroyer which sank with a number of primed depth charges. These charges exploded under the bows of the liner. During the ensuing panic two lifeboats were swamped and 15 people lost their lives. The vessel herself managed to make Plymouth where she was repaired and later returned to service. Immediately after the Armistice the KENILWORTH CASTLE made a voyage to Australia repatriating troops and then returned to the Cape mail service. In 1930 she was chosen, above several bigger and more modern vessels, to carry the Prince of Wales (later King Edward VIII and Duke of Windsor) to South Africa. She was withdrawn and sold for scrap in 1936.

🙶 **ARMADALE CASTLE**   12 973 grt
🙶 **KENILWORTH CASTLE**   12 975 grt   173,8m x 19,7m

Passengers carried in three classes.
Built: Armadale C: Fairfield Co. Ltd., Glasgow, 1903.
Kenilworth C: Harland and Wolff Ltd., Belfast, 1904.
Quadruple expansion engines, coal burning, twin screw, 17 knots.

The DUNLUCE CASTLE and DURHAM CASTLE were two of a class of three vessels built for the intermediate service in 1904. Their sister, the DOVER CASTLE, was torpedoed and sunk with the loss of six lives on 26 May 1917, while serving as a hospital ship in the Mediterranean.

The DUNLUCE CASTLE, after taking troops to England from South Africa in 1914, was also taken up as a hospital ship and served in that capacity for the rest of World War I. She served in the Gallipoli campaign and was on loan to the Italian government for a short time. She later carried wounded and malarial cases from East Africa to Durban and returned to her normal service in 1920. The DURHAM CASTLE remained on the South African run as a mail steamer throughout the war.

Despite being rather tender vessels, the DUNLUCE CASTLE and DURHAM CASTLE were popular with travellers and held their own against the newer vessels which came into service in the 1920s and 1930s. In 1931 they were transferred to the round-Africa service where they were as popular as they had been on the intermediate run. They were withdrawn and sold for scrap in 1939, but before work on them could begin World War II broke out and the British Admiralty stepped in and bought them for service as depot ships.

On 26 January 1940, while on her way to Scapa Flow under tow, the DURHAM CASTLE struck a mine off Cromarty, north east Scotland, and sank. The DUNLUCE CASTLE saw out the war as a depot ship and later as an accommodation vessel in Scapa Flow. In 1945 she was sold and broken up at Inverkeithing.

DUNLUCE CASTLE

DOVER CASTLE

| DUNLUCE CASTLE | 8 130 grt | |
| DURHAM CASTLE | 8 239 grt | 144,9m x 17,3m |

Passengers carried in two classes.
Built: Dunluce C: Harland and Wolff Ltd., Belfast, 1904.
Durham C: Fairfield Co. Ltd., Glasgow, 1904.
Quadruple expansion engines, coal burning, twin screw, 14 knots.

EDINBURGH CASTLE

Though nearly twice the size of the Union liner NORMAN, built in 1894, the BALMORAL CASTLE and EDINBURGH CASTLE were basically modifications of the NORMAN's design, a design which had been used for three other Union liners, two Castle liners and four vessels after the amalgamation, a great compliment to the designer. The design, too, lent itself very well to royal livery as was seen in 1910 when the BALMORAL CASTLE was commissioned as a royal yacht to take the Duke and Duchess of Connaught to Cape Town for the opening of the first Union Parliament. In white with yellow funnels, the BALMORAL CASTLE was a beautiful sight.

At the outbreak of World War I, the BALMORAL CASTLE was not at first requisitioned for war service and remained on the normal mail run until 1917. She was taken up that year and began trooping between the United States and Europe. She made a trooping voyage to Australia shortly after the war and returned to the mail service in 1919.

The EDINBURGH CASTLE was commissioned as an armed merchant cruiser soon after the outbreak of war and served for the most part on the eastern seaboard of South America, spending the last year of the war on convoy duties in the North Atlantic. She, too, returned to the mail service in 1919.

Both vessels reached the end of their commercial lives in 1939 and were sold for scrap. World War II gave the EDINBURGH CASTLE a new lease of life, but was too late to save the BALMORAL CASTLE, the dismantling of which was too far advanced. The EDINBURGH CASTLE was taken over by the British Admiralty for use as an accommodation vessel at Freetown, Sierra Leone, where she rode at anchor in this service until September 1945, when she was sunk by gun fire about 60 nautical miles off the port.

● **BALMORAL CASTLE**   13 361 grt
● **EDINBURGH CASTLE**   13 330 grt   173,8m x 19,7m

Passengers carried in three classes.
Built: Balmoral C: Fairfield Co. Ltd., Glasgow, 1910.
Edinburgh C: Harland and Wolff Ltd., Belfast, 1910.
Quadruple expansion engines, coal burning, twin screw, 17 knots.

108

The GARTH CASTLE was the last vessel ordered by Sir Donald Currie before his death in 1909. It was named after his home in Perthshire in Scotland.

This class was both smaller and slower than the D Class of 1904, and probably for that reason were never as popular with the travelling public. They were nevertheless comfortable for their size, and had, in the opinion of many people, a more pleasing appearance.

Both vessels had rather uneventful careers, the GARTH CASTLE being a hospital ship attached to the Grand Fleet at Scapa Flow, Cromarty Firth and the Firth of Forth throughout World War I. At first the GRANTULLY CASTLE was used as a troop transport and in this role was present at the first landings in the Dardanelles. From June 1915 to April 1919 she served, first as a hospital ship and later as an ambulance ship on the Cross-Channel service between France and England.

The GARTH CASTLE came into the news in 1926 when in March that year she 'collided' with Ascension Island. Her passengers had to be transferred to the KENILWORTH CASTLE, and the GARTH CASTLE, her forward hold flooded and down by the head by about 2,5 metres, made her way to Cape Town for repairs.

The GRANTULLY CASTLE was laid up in reserve in 1930 but was brought back into service in 1933 to replace the GUILDFORD CASTLE which had been lost in a collision in the River Elbe.

Both vessels were withdrawn from service in 1939 and were scrapped shortly before the outbreak of World War II.

GARTH CASTLE

GARTH CASTLE   7 715 grt
GRANTULLY CASTLE   7 612 grt
137,9 (Grantully C 137,4) m x 16,6m
Passengers carried in three, later two, classes.
Built: Barclay, Curle and Co. Ltd., Glasgow, 1910.
Quadruple expansion engines, coal burning, twin screw, 13 knots.

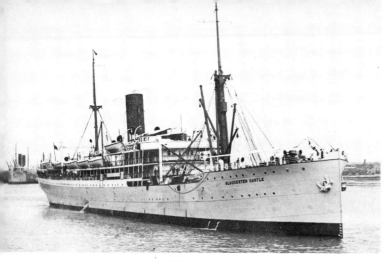

GLOUCESTER CASTLE

The GLOUCESTER CASTLE was the sole survivor of a class of three vessels brought into service in 1911. Of her two sisters, the GALWAY CASTLE, after having been used on the regular mail service between the United Kingdom and South Africa throughout World War I, was torpedoed and sunk on 12 September 1918, with considerable loss of life; the other vessel, the GUILDFORD CASTLE, having come through the war unscathed, was in collision in the River Elbe in Germany with the Blue Funnel liner STENTOR on 1 June 1933, and became a total loss.

During World War I the GLOUCESTER CASTLE had a narrow escape while serving as a hospital ship. On 31 March 1917 she was torpedoed with the loss of three lives. However, her bulkheads held and she was able to make Southampton where she was eventually repaired and returned to service.

She returned to company service in 1920 and was put on the round-Africa service until 1926 when she reverted to the west coast intermediate run.

Withdrawn from service in 1939, she was brought out of reserve on the outbreak of World War II and placed on the mail run to South Africa. On 15 July 1942, while on a voyage from Liverpool to Table Bay, she was shelled and sunk by the German commerce raider MICHEL off the coast of South West Africa. Her captain and 92 of the passengers and crew were killed; a further 61 people were taken prisoner and landed in Japan, where two later died in captivity. The fate of the GLOUCESTER CASTLE did not become known for quite some time as one of the first shells had destroyed her radio. The MICHEL was torpedoed and sunk, with great loss of life, on 17 October 1943, by the United States submarine TARPON.

GALWAY
GUILDFORD

● **GLOUCESTER CASTLE**   7 999 grt   138m x 17,1m
Passengers carried in three, later two, classes.
Built: Fairfield Co. Ltd., Glasgow, 1911.
Quadruple expansion coal burning engines, twin screw, 13 knots.

At the time that this vessel was built, the chairman of the company, Sir Owen Philipps, was the Lord of the Manor of Llanstephan in Wales, hence the name which the vessel bore in the company service for 38 years.

The LLANSTEPHAN CASTLE was the second vessel to be given a Llan name, the first was her sister, the LLANDOVERY CASTLE of ill-fated memory.

Both vessels were built for the new East Coast Royal Mail service, and the LLANSTEPHAN CASTLE had completed only one commercial voyage before the outbreak of World War I.

Neither vessel was taken up for war service until 1917, though they replaced mail steamers in the west coast service. The LLANSTEPHAN CASTLE was taken over for trooping between the United States and France in 1917, and the LLANDOVERY CASTLE became a hospital ship at the same time.

The LLANDOVERY CASTLE achieved notoriety in this service when she was torpedoed, with her Red Crosses brightly lit, in the North Atlantic. It was a calm evening, 27 June 1918, and most of the 258 passengers and crew got away in the boats. However, the submarine, U 86, surfaced and shelled the boats, sinking all but one of them. The 24 men and women in this boat were the only survivors. The matter became the subject of a war criminal trial after the war.

The LLANSTEPHAN CASTLE survived the war and returned to her normal role. In 1919 she brought General Louis Botha back to South Africa after the signing of the Treaty of Versailles. After that she lapsed into a placid and

LLANSTEPHAN CASTLE

LLANDOVERY

● **LLANSTEPHAN CASTLE**   11 293 grt   152,5m x 19,3m
Passengers carried in three, later two, classes.
Built: Fairfield Co. Ltd., Glasgow, 1914.
Quadruple expansion engines, coal burning until 1939 when converted to oil, twin screw, 15 knots.

regular routine until, in 1939, the world was once again at war.

In 1940 she brought the first 300 child evacuees to South Africa, and the next year was commodore vessel in the first of the Russian Arctic convoys. Later she served in the Royal Indian Navy as a support ship and took part in the Burma campaign.

In September 1947 she restarted the round-Africa service but the writing was on the wall for the old lady. In 1952 new vessels came from the builders' yards and the LLANSTE-PHAN CASTLE, after a career of 38 years, the longest of any vessel in the Union Castle Company's history, was sold to British shipbreakers.

Shortly after the Union Castle Company was taken over by Lord Kylsant's Royal Mail group, a new mail steamer was ordered, to be almost half as big again as any liner then on the service. The keel was laid down in 1915, but the needs of World War I intervened and building was delayed until after the war. The vessel, named ARUNDEL CASTLE, finally came into service in 1921. About the time that work was resumed on the ARUNDEL CASTLE, a sister was ordered from John Brown's in Glasgow. Her launching as the WINDSOR CASTLE by the Prince of Wales, later King Edward VIII and Duke of Windsor, is believed to have been the first time a merchant vessel was launched by a member of Britain's Royal Family since King James VI and I of Scotland and England launched an East Indiaman in the early 17th century.

The two vessels were of a design completely different from any that had previously been seen on the Cape run. Apart from their size, their four tall funnels set them aside from any other vessel calling at South African ports. They were different internally too. They were the first turbine driven vessels in the mail service and their interior fittings too, were greatly in advance of earlier steamers. But they were not beautiful to look at; they were too short for the grace and power of the four-funnellers of the North Atlantic. For all that, they proved popular in the Cape trade, and, in 1936, when an accelerated mail service was introduced, were considered worth rebuilding.

Though they had come from different yards initially, the rebuilding and re-engining of both liners was undertaken by Harland and Wolff who produced two really beautiful vessels, both 201,6 metres long, with two graceful funnels in place of the four tall thin uptakes. In the lengthening, each was given a fine semi-clipper stem, which really did give the

ARUNDEL CASTLE

○ **ARUNDEL CASTLE**   19 023 grt   192,2m x 22,1m
○ **WINDSOR CASTLE**   18 967 grt   192,7m x 22,1m
Passengers carried in three, later two, classes.
Built: Arundel C — Harland and Wolff Ltd., Belfast, 1921.
Windsor C — John Brown and Co. Ltd., Glasgow, 1922.
Four steam turbines, twin screw, 16 knots.

impression of power and speed.

Their tonnages were increased to 19 118 and 19 141 grt respectively.

World War II saw both vessels taken up for trooping duties, and while in this service, the WINDSOR CASTLE met her end. On 23 March 1943, when 90 miles north west of Algiers, she was torpedoed by a German aircraft. Six men lost their lives, but the 3 000 troops on board were transferred to escorting vessels without further loss. The crippled vessel was taken in tow, but some hours later she settled by the stern and, shortly after her master and skeleton crew had abandoned ship, she went down.

The ARUNDEL CASTLE was more fortunate. She carried on throughout the war as a troop transport, and after hostilities had ceased was one of three mail vessels chartered by the Union government to ferry immigrants from the United Kingdom to South Africa. She returned to normal service in 1950. Even though outclassed by the newer mail steamers, she remained a popular vessel and gave good service for a further nine years. It was not until 1959, some 48 years after her keel had been laid, that the ARUNDEL CASTLE finally bowed out and was sent to the scrapyard.

The only four-funnelled vessels in regular service to South Africa, both the ARUNDEL CASTLE and the WINDSOR CASTLE proved popular ships with the travelling public. After rebuilding they were also among the most beautiful liners seen in South African ports.

As different from her immediate predecessors as they had been from their's, the CARNARVON CASTLE was a vessel of firsts. She was the first motor vessel to enter the South African mail service; she was the first Union Castle liner to exceed 20 000 tons gross; and later she was the first of the company's vessels to be commissioned into the Royal Navy in World War II.

When she came out in 1926 she had a straight stem, cruiser stern and two rather unsightly squat funnels. She was a comfortable ship, but was not at first able to break into the popularity of the older steam vessels.

In 1936 the CARNARVON CASTLE, together with four other liners, was sent back to her builders for rebuilding. When she came out of their yards, the transformation was almost unbelievable. Gone were the two squat funnels and in their place was one graceful pear-shaped funnel. Her straight stem had been replaced by one of semi-clipper design, and she had been lengthened by 9,3 metres. Her speed had been increased to 20 knots by re-engining, so that she could take her place in the new accelerated mail service. On her first voyage after modification she did the voyage from the Nab Tower to Cape Town breakwater in 12 days, 13 hours and 38 minutes, setting a record which was not broken until the new EDINBURGH CASTLE did the voyage in 11 days, 21 hours from Plymouth in 1954.

The CARNARVON CASTLE was in South African waters when World War II broke out. She was immediately destored in Cape Town and sent to Simonstown for fitting out as an armed merchant cruiser. She was commissioned as HMS

CARNAVON CASTLE

CARNARVON CASTLE   20 063 grt   192,2m x 22,4m
Passengers carried in three, later two, classes.
Built: Harland and Wolff Ltd., Belfast, 1926.
Diesel, twin screw, 16 knots.

CARNARVON CASTLE on 8 September 1939. Three months later she engaged the German commerce raider THOR in the South Atlantic, but her armament of pre-World War I guns were not up to fighting a modern enemy and the German ship escaped unscathed. The CARNARVON CASTLE's damage was repaired at Montevideo — with plating recovered from the wreck of the German battleship ADMIRAL GRAF SPEE.

She served for most of the war as an auxiliary cruiser, and in 1944 was converted for trooping duties. After hostilities ceased, the CARNARVON CASTLE was one of the vessels used to bring immigrants to South Africa, and did not return to her normal service until June 1950. After this her career was uneventful and, in 1962, she was sold to Japanese shipbreakers. She arrived at Mihara for breaking up on 8 September that year, exactly 23 years after her commissioning into the Royal Navy, and a little more than 36 years after her maiden voyage.

An ugly duckling when she came out, she later developed into a graceful swan and one of the most popular mail vessels ever on the South African service.

Two 'Llans' were built in the mid 1920s for the round-Africa service. They were modifications of the LLANSTEPHAN CASTLE class, but were slightly smaller and had one deck less. The LLANDOVERY CASTLE was named after the hospital ship which had been sunk in World War I.

Popular vessels with wide and airy accommodation, ideally suited to tropical voyaging, the LLANDAFF CASTLE and LLANDOVERY CASTLE were popular vessels, particularly on the East Coast of Africa. Both vessels were taken up for trooping on the outbreak of World War II and spent a good deal of their wartime service between Durban and ports on the Red Sea. The LLANDAFF CASTLE, while bringing troops and prisoners of war from the north to South Africa, was torpedoed about 100 miles south of Maputo on 30 November 1942. There was heavy loss of life among the crew, troops and prisoners of war.

The LLANDOVERY CASTLE returned to her normal service after the war, but was withdrawn in 1952 when three new vessels were brought out for the service. She was disposed of for scrap during the same year.

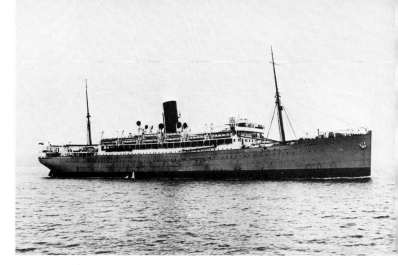

LLANDAFF CASTLE

LLANDAFF CASTLE   10 786 grt
LLANDOVERY CASTLE   10 640 grt
143,6m x 18,8m
Passengers carried in three, later two, classes.
Built: Llandovery C — Barclay, Curle and Co. Ltd., Glasgow, 1925.
Llandaff C — Workman, Clark and Co. Ltd., Belfast, 1926.
Quadruple expansion engines, coal burning until 1939, then oil burning, 14 knots.

117

LLANGIBBY CASTLE

The first motor liner designed for the intermediate service, the LLANGIBBY CASTLE was a truly 'United Kingdom' vessel — built by an Irish firm, in their Scottish yard, for an English company, to carry a Welsh name.

In appearance a smaller edition of the CARNARVON CASTLE, she was, if anything, even less graceful. Her funnels — she was the first two-funnelled intermediate liner — were set too far forward to allow for a balanced silhouette. Her passenger accommodation, though, was superior to anything yet seen on that service. For all this, she was never quite as popular as the earlier intermediates or round-Africa liners. Perhaps prospective travellers were put off by her appearance — appearance being very important at that time.

She served as a troop transport during World War II, and had an uneventful career in this role until 16 January 1942, when she was torpedoed, the torpedo hitting her in the stern and blowing off her rudder. She was carrying 1 400 troops at the time, but the casualities were restricted mainly to the gunners on board who were quartered in the poop. The LLANGIBBY CASTLE did not sink and made her way, first to Horta in the Azores, and then to Gibraltar, using only her twin screws for motive power and steering. After 14 days at Horta and a period under repair at Gibraltar, the vessel made it back to the United Kingdom, unescorted for most of the way.

The saving of the LLANGIBBY CASTLE was one of the great stories of seamanship to come out of World War II.

Later the LLANGIBBY CASTLE served in the North African, Sicilian and Normandy landings.

She returned to her normal passenger service after the war until she was sold for breaking up in 1954.

LLANGIBBY CASTLE   11 951 grt   148m x 20,2m
Passengers carried in two classes.
Built: Harland and Wolff Ltd., Govan, 1929.
Diesel engines, twin screw, 15 knots.

Modifications of the CARNARVON CASTLE design, these two vessels, for some undefinable reason, appeared more graceful than their predecessor. They were not on the mail service very long when the new mail contract, negotiated in the mid-1930s, demanded a faster service. Both vessels were returned to their builders for re-engining and modifications to bring them up to the standard required by the new contract. Their funnels were removed and replaced with a single funnel of more graceful proportions. Their hulls, however, were untouched; they had been built with much finer lines than the CARNARVON CASTLE and did not require alterations to give them the necessary extra speed.

They were among the most comfortable vessels ever to serve South Africa, and many people still remember the Spanish decor of the first class public rooms of the WINCHESTER CASTLE, and the high degree of comfort in her tourist class lounge. Many considered the public rooms of the subsequent mail vessels as cold when compared with those in these two liners.

Like most big liners, they were taken up for trooping in World War II and it was during this service that the WARWICK CASTLE was lost. On 14 November 1942, while returning to the United Kingdom after the North African landings, the WARWICK CASTLE was torpedoed by a German U-boat. The captain and 62 officers and men lost their lives. The WARWICK CASTLE sank in about 20 minutes, a very short time for a vessel of her size.

The WINCHESTER CASTLE was used during the later part of the war as an assault training vessel for troops to be engaged in the invasion of Normandy. After the war she was used for a while to take immigrants to South Africa, and later returned to the normal mail service. She was sold for breaking up in 1960.

WINCHESTER CASTLE

| WARWICK CASTLE | 20 445 grt |
| WINCHESTER CASTLE | 20 109 grt |

198,6(Winchester C 192,5)m x 23m
Passengers carried in three, later two, classes.
Built: Harland and Wolff Ltd., Belfast, 1930.
Diesel engines, twin screw, 16 knots.

DUNBAR CASTLE

The DUNBAR CASTLE was a smaller edition of the LLAN-GIBBY CASTLE and was built for the same service. Her accommodation was an improvement on that of the earlier vessel, and in service she was more popular. She suffered, though, from a very similar silhouette.

On 9 January 1940 she became the first war loss of the Union Castle Company. She was outward bound from London for Beira when she struck a mine north east of the North Goodwin Sands, and sank in 30 minutes. The captain was fatally injured when the foremast, broken by the explosion, fell across the bridge. He died later in one of the lifeboats. One other man was killed and seven were missing.

The survivors were later picked up and landed in England by a coastal motor barge.

For many years the DUNBAR CASTLE, which had settled in shallow water on an even keel, could be seen, looking for all the world as though she was just waiting to be pumped dry and taken to port. However, her back was broken and she was too greatly damaged below to be salvaged. The wreck was blown up and dismantled after the war.

DUNBAR CASTLE   10 002 grt   143,6m x 18,7m
Passengers carried in two classes.
Built: Harland and Wolff Ltd., Govan, 1930.
Diesel engines, twin screw, 15 knots.

120

Considered by many to have been among the most graceful liners ever built, the ATHLONE CASTLE and STIRLING CASTLE were the first mail vessels in a programme demanded by the faster mail service which came into operation in 1938.

Both were taken up for trooping service immediately World War II broke out, and the following year the ATHLONE CASTLE was commodore ship in one of the first big troop convoys which passed through South African ports on their way from the United Kingdom to the Middle East. Later in the war these liners were used to ferry troops from the United States to Britain before the invasion of Normandy. As troopships, each could carry about 6 000 troops with equipment. Their contribution to the war effort and subsequent victory was almost incalculable.

The ATHLONE CASTLE and STIRLING CASTLE were among the first liners to return to normal service in the South African mail run. In this they continued until a faster mail service was required, a service demanding a speed of which they were incapable. It was a sad sight to see these two liners sail out of Table Bay for the last time, particularly for those who remembered their coming. The ATHLONE CASTLE, in December 1938, inaugurated the then new 13½-day mail service; in November 1965 her sister, the STIRLING CASTLE took the last sailing of that service. The record-breakers of the 1930s were too slow for the service in the 1960s. The ATHLONE CASTLE was broken up in 1966; the STIRLING CASTLE followed her to the shipbreakers the following year.

STIRLING CASTLE

ATHLONE CASTLE   25 564 grt
STIRLING CASTLE   25 550 grt
212,1m x 25,1m
Passengers carried in two classes.
Built: Harland and Wolff Ltd., Belfast, 1936.
Diesel engines, twin screw, 20 knots.

DUNVEGAN CASTLE

When these two vessels appeared, they brought a new standard of passenger accommodation into the intermediate service. Built for the round-Africa service, they were used on the mail run for a while when the older mail vessels were being rebuilt and re-engined.

The outbreak of World War II interrupted the service in which the DUNNOTTAR CASTLE and DUNVEGAN CASTLE were engaged, and the two liners were requisitioned by the British government for service as auxiliary cruisers. The DUNVEGAN CASTLE was torpedoed and sunk in this service, while on patrol off the west coast of Ireland. Four officers and 23 ratings were killed when the vessel was hit on 28 August 1940. The survivors, 250 in number, were landed in Scotland.

The DUNNOTTAR CASTLE was later converted to a troop transport and returned to her normal service after the war.

In 1958 the DUNNOTTAR CASTLE was withdrawn from service; the trade on the east coast of Africa had dropped off after the independence of those African states. She was put up for sale and was bought by Incres Shipping Company who carried out a remarkable and extensive conversion. The vessel was given new bows and stem, a new stern; she was re-engined and given a new more streamlined funnel; and, of course, her accommodation was completely redesigned and rebuilt. Lastly, she was given a new name, VICTORIA. She started her cruising career in 1959.

Sold again, she was laid up for a while in 1974, but towards the end of 1975 she was bought by Chandris Lines, refuge of a number of other old Union Castle liners, and has since been seen in South African waters as a luxury cruise ship. More than 40 years old now, she seems good for many years yet.

DUNNOTTAR CASTLE   ● DUNVEGAN CASTLE

15 007 grt   164,5m x 21,9m

Passengers carried in two classes.

Built: Harland and Wolff Ltd., Belfast, 1936.

Diesel engines, twin screw, 16 knots.

122

A larger modification of the ATHLONE CASTLE class, the CAPETOWN CASTLE was the first vessel in the Union Castle fleet to have been named after a castle not in the United Kingdom. She entered the mail service in 1938 as flagship of the company and ran on the run until the outbreak of World War II, when she was requisitioned as a troop transport. During this period, she was seen in almost every port in the Allied countries, and was the only South African mail service liner ever to pass through the Straits of Magellan — on a voyage which took her from Cape Town, through the Straits, up the west coast of South America, through the Panama Canal, and up the east coast of the United States to New York.

She returned to the mail service after the war and remained until she was withdrawn in 1965 when the new accelerated mail service came into operation. From then until her final departure she was used as an 'extra' vessel, running one-class only voyages on a 16-day service between the United Kingdom and Cape Town. She was withdrawn from service in 1967 and sold for breaking up.

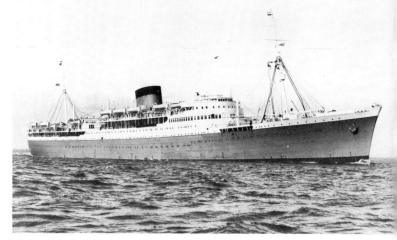

CAPETOWN CASTLE

CAPETOWN CASTLE   27 002 grt   214,2m x 25,1m
Passengers carried in two classes.
Built: Harland and Wolff Ltd., Belfast, 1938.
Diesel engines, twin screw, 20 knots.

DURBAN CASTLE

Said by some to have been the most successful intermediate liners ever built for the Union Castle Company, these two fine vessels appeared shortly before World War II. The PRETORIA CASTLE, in fact, had completed only a few voyages when she was taken up as an armed merchant cruiser in November 1939.

With these two vessels, the company introduced a custom which they followed for some years afterwards, that of naming their vessels after non-existent castles. Nevertheless, the inhabitants of Durban and Pretoria felt duly honoured, which was probably the idea behind the company's naming policy.

The DURBAN CASTLE became a troop transport during World War II, in which role she gave sterling service. The career of the PRETORIA CASTLE was more varied. After serving as an auxiliary cruiser until 1943, she was bought outright by the British Admiralty who sent her to her builders for conversion to an escort carrier. Her speed was not sufficient for this role, and she was used from then until the end of the war as a training carrier.

After the war, Union Castle bought back the PRETORIA CASTLE, renamed her WARWICK CASTLE, after the mail vessel lost in 1942, and put her back into service with her sister, the DURBAN CASTLE, which had been refitted after her war service.

With the fall-off of trade in East Africa, these two fine vessels became surplus to requirements and in 1962 both were withdrawn from service. As no buyers came forward to take them for further trading, they were disposed of for breaking up.

DURBAN CASTLE   17 388 grt
PRETORIA CASTLE (later WARWICK CASTLE)
17 392 grt   181,2m x 23,3m
Passengers carried in two classes.
Built: Harland and Wolff Ltd., Belfast, 1938, 1939.
Diesel engines, twin screw, 17 knots.

The EDINBURGH CASTLE was the second mail steamer built by Union Castle after World War II. Her sister, the PRETORIA CASTLE, later transferred to the South African Marine Corporation and renamed SA ORANJE, was the first. The two vessels were built to replace the WARWICK CASTLE and WINDSOR CASTLE which were lost during the war.

As she was built so soon after the war and before Britain had got out of her austerity mood, she was not as lavishly fitted out as her predecessors had been. Nevertheless, she was a comfortable vessel, though vibration in the after accommodation could be felt rather strongly whenever the vessel was required to put on speed. The EDINBURGH CASTLE had a trouble-free career of nearly 30 years, missing only one voyage when she was taken out of service for modification when her hull was plasticised, her accommodation updated, her masts removed and a small signal mast stepped just abaft the bridge. This outward alteration did not improve her appearance, which was already somewhat marred by the large funnel necessary for a steamship.

The EDINBURGH CASTLE was withdrawn from service in April 1976, and shortly afterwards made her way to Taiwan where she was broken up for scrap.

EDINBURGH CASTLE

EDINBURGH CASTLE   28 705 grt   227,8m x 25,6m
Passengers carried in two classes.
Built: Harland and Wolff Ltd., Belfast, 1948.
Six steam turbines, twin screw, 22 knots.

BLOEMFONTEIN CASTLE

The BLOEMFONTEIN CASTLE was the first one-class passenger liner built by the Union Castle Company. She was intended for the service out by the west coast, up the east coast to Beira, from where she would return to the United Kingdom by the west coast route, and she remained on this route for most of her career. There were teething troubles when she first came out, earning her the unflattering nickname 'Bedlam Castle'. These troubles were later ironed out, but nevertheless her career in the fleet was comparatively short. The company sold her when she was only nine years old.

She came into prominence in January 1953 when she rescued the survivors of the Holland Afrika Lijn vessel KLIPFONTEIN which had struck a rock and foundered off the Mozambique coast.

In 1959 she was bought by Chandris Lines who sent her to the Tyne for an overhaul before putting her onto their service between European ports and Australia. They gave her the name PATRIS. Later in her career she went cruising from Australian ports, and in 1976 was converted to a passenger-car ferry for service between Italy and Greece.

BLOEMFONTEIN CASTLE   18 400 grt   181,2m x 23,3m
Passengers carried in one class only.
Built: Harland and Wolff Ltd., Belfast, 1950.
Diesel engines, twin screw, 18,5 knots.

These three vessels were the last intermediate liners built for the round-Africa service. They did not differ much in appearance from the lines of the BLOEMFONTEIN CASTLE, but they were a great improvement inside. Their engines, too, were less inclined to give trouble.

The first interruption in their service came in 1956 when the Suez Canal was closed during one of the Arab-Israeli wars. The fall-off of the passenger trade from East Africa also affected the vessels, and by the early 1960s Union Castle Company were rethinking the future of these vessels.

First to go was the BRAEMAR CASTLE after a career of only 13 years, the shortest career of a Union Castle liner before being scrapped. She was broken up in Faslane, Scotland in 1966. The RHODESIA CASTLE, oldest of the trio, went to Taiwanese shipbreakers the following year, and at about the same time the KENYA CASTLE was sold to the Chandris Lines who refitted her as a cruise ship and renamed her AMERIKANIS. The KENYA CASTLE was the last intermediate liner operated by the Union Castle Company, and with her departure from the scene a service going back more than 100 years came to an end.

KENYA CASTLE

BRAEMAR CASTLE	17 029 grt	
KENYA CASTLE	17 041 grt	
RHODESIA CASTLE	17 041 grt	175,7m x 22,7m

Passengers carried in one class only.
Built: Harland and Wolff Ltd., Belfast, 1952, 1952, 1951.
Six steam turbines, twin screw, 17 knots.

127

PENDENNIS CASTLE

The only vessel to carry this name in Union Castle history, the PENDENNIS CASTLE was building when Union Castle Company and Clan Line Steamers formed the British and Commonwealth shipping group in 1957. Her building was held up for some time while alterations were made to the plans. In the end a very different vessel emerged from Harland and Wolff's Belfast yards than had originally been intended. She was also the last of a long line of passenger liners built by Harland and Wolff for the Union Castle Company, and ended an association between the two companies which went back to the days before the amalgamation of the Union Line and the Castle Packets Company in 1900.

An odd-man-out in the fleet in more ways than just not having a sistership, the PENDENNIS CASTLE was nevertheless a relatively popular vessel. When she came out the future appeared to hold a reasonably long career for her. However, in the event, oil sheiks and seamen's unions changed that, and by 1976 it was proving increasingly difficult to run passenger liners at a profit, in fact, it was becoming impossible. When, then, it was announced in early 1976 that the PENDENNIS CASTLE was to be withdrawn and offered for sale, many were sorry but few were surprised.

She left Table Bay on her last northbound voyage on 2 June 1976. The following month she left Southampton for the Phillipines where she was to be refitted as a cruise ship. Her new owners renamed her OCEAN QUEEN, painted her all-over white and painted the funnel completely red. The new livery does not spoil her lines, but at the time of writing she has still to make a cruise with passengers.

● **PENDENNIS CASTLE**   27 109 grt   232,6m x 25,6m
Passengers carried in two classes.
Built: Harland and Wolff Ltd., Belfast, 1958.
Two steam turbines, twin screw, 22 knots.

WINDSOR CASTLE

The largest liner built for the South African mail passenger service, the WINDSOR CASTLE was launched by H.M. Queen Elizabeth, the Queen Mother, and was the first Cape mail steamer to be built away from Belfast since her namesake was launched by the Queen Mother's brother-in-law in 1921.

Beautifully appointed, air-conditioned and stabilized, the WINDSOR CASTLE was all that could be asked of a passenger liner. In July 1965, she inaugurated the new 11-day mail service, and on her outward voyage passed the ATHLONE CASTLE, one of the last 13½-day service vessels, on her last homeward voyage, a poignant meeting. With the withdrawal of the WINDSOR CASTLE in September 1977, an end came to the passenger mail service between the United Kingdom and South Africa which had started with the departure for the Cape of the General Screw Ship Company's BOSPHORUS in December 1850. A tradition has passed.

WINDSOR CASTLE   34 149 grt   238,7m x 28,2m
Passengers carried in two classes.
Built: Cammell, Laird and Co. Ltd., Birkenhead, 1960.
Four steam turbines, twin screw, 22 knots.

INDEX